Little Guide to
PROTECTION MAGIC

Everything You Need to Know
Including Protection Spells

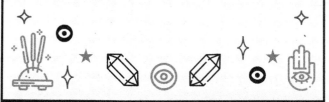

PRACTICAL MAGIC SERIES
TESS WHITEHURST

Little Guide to Protection Magic © 2021 by Tess Whitehurst.
Book 2 in Tess Whitehurst's Practical Magic series.
All rights reserved.

Cover design: Monarose Ryan
thepinklibrarian.com

Tess Whitehurst believes life is magical. In addition to writing lots of books and articles about magical living, she's the founder and facilitator of the Good Vibe Tribe Online School of Magical Arts, the co-creator of the *Your Most Magical Year Yet!* planner series, and the co-host of Magic Monday Podcast. Learn more about Tess, sign up for her newsletter, and read her blog at tesswhitehurst.com.

Practical Magic Series

Little Guide to Love Magic

Little Guide to Protection Magic

Coming Soon

Little Guide to Money Magic

Little Guide to House Magic

Little Guide to Success Magic

Little Guide to Chakra Magic

Life shrinks or expands in proportion to one's courage.

~ Anaïs Nin

Contents
◉ ◉ ◉

Introduction   *1*

1. Establish Equanimity   5
The Violet Fire   8
Hand It Over   13

2. Align with the Divine   17
Get Your House in Order   20
Basic Home Protection Ritual   22
A Fierce Aura   23

3. Angelic Forces   29
Archangel Michael   32
Archangel Raphael   33
Archangel Chamuel   34
Archangel Zaphkiel   36
Angelic Tune-In Ritual   37

4. Basic Protection Techniques   43
Radiate   44
Shield   47
Deflect   49
Cloak   51

5. Amulets   55
Minerals   57
Botanicals   63
Charms, Symbols, and Other Materials   69

6. Spells & Rituals   77
How to Cast a Circle   78
How to Release a Circle   81
Spells and Rituals to Protect Yourself   83
Spells and Rituals to Protect Your Loved Ones   94
Spells and Rituals to Protect Your Stuff   97

Conclusion   101
Bibliography   103

Introduction

Welcome to the *Little Guide to Protection Magic*!

Spiritual protection is an essential prerequisite for any magical act, just as taking care of your physical, mental, and emotional self is a universal value and aim.

A need for protection is not synonymous with a need for fear, alarm, or panic. Protection magic is about acknowledging that there are dangers in the world while also consciously cultivating an abiding sense of empowerment and calm.

Protection magic does not ask us to *deny* our fear. Fear is a part of being human. We don't need to shame ourselves for feeling fear or to pretend the source of our fear doesn't exist. Putting your seat belt on before driving and wearing a mask during a global pandemic are wise choices, not fearful ones, even though they stem from the (healthy) fears of being injured in an accident and spreading a potentially deadly disease. Instead of wallowing in such fears, or denying that we feel them at all, we're putting them to good use when we take simple steps to protect ourselves.

The same is true of protection magic. Taking action to protect yourself is a wise thing to do and can help you to be safer on all levels, which, in turn, will transform your fear into strength. (We'll talk more about transforming fear in chapter 1.)

Speaking of things like seat belts and masks, keep in mind as you read that protection magic should be approached holistically. Whenever possible, be sure to use protection magic in tandem with commonsense protective measures in the physical world. No matter how many home protection spells you've cast, don't say, "I don't need to lock my doors at night because I'm protected by magic!" For Goddess's sake, help magic out a little. Lock your doors.

Also keep in mind that as you work with the principles and practices in this book, you may notice your personal boundaries becoming clearer and more defined. For example, you may notice that you have one or more relationships or responsibilities that don't feel great to you. If this happens, don't worry. Just ask yourself what you need to shift in order to protect your personal energy and safeguard your authenticity. There may be a truth you need to speak or a guideline you need to set. Be aware that as you hone your protection magic skills, some relationships and situations may change and others may end. This is all part of the healthy process of learning to take meticulous care of yourself in both the visible and invisible realms.

But do be sure to get help when you need it. For example, if you live with an abusive partner, you may need to call a domestic violence hotline for help with getting yourself out of the house safely and out of harm's way. Or, even if a relationship isn't violent or obsessive, you may want to talk to a therapist for help with shifting it, ending it, or (if you're not sure yet, but you know something needs to change) simply getting clarity on it.

Magic doesn't exist in a vacuum. As powerful as magic can be, you still need to take real-world action to get yourself out of unhealthy relationships and untenable situations. I bring this up because I have received a number of questions over the years from people who think magic might be able to save them from having to make necessary changes in their lives. Like if they just do a protection spell, their abusive partner is going to magically stop being abusive, or the abuse somehow isn't going to harm them anymore. I can certainly sympathize. In such a situation, your energy and self-protection instincts would be worn down, and leaving any close relationship is painful, no matter how terrible it is. Regardless, necessary changes are still necessary. When performed correctly, protection magic will support you in making such necessary changes. But first, it may make their necessity more pronounced. While I can't promise that any of this will be easy, it will ultimately bring you greater mastery over your life than ever before.

In this book, you will learn to align with divinity and tap into divine power so you can feel safe wherever you go. It will empower you to wake up in the morning knowing you can courageously face and gracefully navigate whatever happens. You'll learn the basics of protection magic, along with useful exercises you can keep in your back pocket for life. You'll meet divine helpers you can call on anytime, discover protective charms and talismans for various purposes, and gain access to a wealth of powerful protection spells that can be employed for a wide range of purposes.

If you want to feel safe, relaxed, and at home in the world, you're in the right place. Congratulations! You've found your way.

Brightest Blessings,
Tess

Chapter 1

Establish Equanimity

When I was five years old, I was afraid of dogs. Actually, just one dog: the neighbor's. It started when I ran by the neighbor's yard on the way home from school and his dog decided to chase me. This became a daily ritual. My mom would say, "That dog only chases you because you run from him." But rather than calming my fear, this only made it worse. Knowing I wasn't supposed to run from the neighbor's dog made me *want* to run! It made me think of nothing *but* running.

Even then, I knew this was a vicious cycle: my fear was actually causing me to call in more of what I was afraid of. But that knowledge didn't do me any good. It only added a layer of frustration to my fear.

I'm not sharing this story so you can marvel at the cavalier parenting techniques and dog care practices of the early 1980s. (I mean, why was I walking home from school by myself at the age of five? And why was there an unattended German shepherd in the neighbor's front yard?) I'm sharing this story because before I tell you rule number one of protection magic, I want you to know that I fully understand that following it isn't quite as easy as it sounds.

So what *is* the first rule of protection magic? *Clear the fear.*

When you establish an inner state of equanimity—serenity, neutrality, and emotional equilibrium—you are in the protection magic strike zone. You are like the rakish star of your own action movie: relaxed, magnetic, and open while also poised to protect yourself at a moment's notice in whatever way is needed. (Think Han Solo or Buffy the Vampire Slayer.)

And, in much the same way that the neighbor's dog probably won't chase you if you don't run from him, your aura of courage will often neutralize potential threats before they begin. Whether you seek to protect yourself from visible forces (such as the neighbor or his dog) or invisible ones (such as a curse or a poltergeist), a vibration of calm is a powerful energetic shield in its own right. That's why clearing the fear is the perfect place for us to start.

Obviously, you will continue to feel fear throughout your lifetime. It's not like you can get rid of it for good, nor would you want to! After all, fear helps you avoid things like wandering too close to the edge of a cliff and plummeting to your death. In many ways, fear is actually protective.

But when fear rules you, it's not protecting you. When you have a free-floating, sort of ill-defined fear, or when everything scares you, or when one thing scares you so much that you can hardly think of anything else, then fear is doing the opposite of protecting you—it's endangering you. It's like running from the neighbor's dog. But even if the thing you fear never happens (which it usually doesn't), the feeling of fear can be its own threat and can create its own terror. It can put you in a place of both inner and outer danger. Come to think of it, President Franklin D. Roosevelt could have been talking about protection magic when he said, "The only thing we have to fear is fear itself."

This can seem like a catch-22. Because if you're going to do protection magic, it's often because, on some level, you're afraid of something. Even if you don't fear something at this very moment, you know you will when the need for protection magic arises. And you also know that the more you try to push the fear away (like five-year-old me with the neighbor's dog), the more fearful you will become. So maybe you're reading this and worrying that you're destined to fail.

But you aren't! Because here's the thing: it's not about erasing or fighting or pushing against the fear; it's about recognizing it, allowing it to be there, and then shifting it into something else. Thoughts, energies, and emotions have a natural emanation and flow, like the wind and the sunlight. You want to tell the wind to blow in a different direction or the sun to go shine somewhere else? Well, you can try, but they won't listen. But what you *can* do is put up some windmills and some solar panels. You can take those natural forces and channel them into something that will work on your behalf and contribute to a momentum of your choosing. You can say, "Oh, here's the fear! Let me acknowledge the power in it and turn it to my benefit." By working *with* the fear's momentum rather than against it, you can learn to rule it: to become its master rather than its servant. Over time, you will stop fearing the fear, which will not only take the edge off but also reduce your total fear quotient by approximately 98 percent.

In many ways, *clear the fear* is not just the first but also the *only* rule of protection magic. All the other stuff in this book—

the spells, the rituals, the crystals, the visualizations, all of it—is about clearing the fear in various ways and establishing a strong force field and reliable momentum of confidence and calm. The more you practice the techniques in this book, the more masterful you will become and the more naturally protected you will be, spiritually, emotionally, mentally, and physically. When you move through the world feeling that you are more than equal to any challenge that may come your way, your aura will shine brightly and you will be a beacon of bright positivity: a human protection amulet. No matter where you go, you will feel safe, and other people will feel safe just by being around you.

The Violet Fire

Here's a reliable tool for neutralizing fear anytime it arises within you. It's called the violet fire, and you can use it anywhere, anytime. The first time you work with the violet fire requires a longer visualization, which you will discover shortly. Afterward, you will be able to access it instantly. I suggest that you record yourself reading the visualization as a voice memo on your phone so you can play it back while you're doing it.

Quick note: until we get to the final chapter (which is a collection of specific rituals for specific situations), I recommend that you do each exercise in the book as you encounter it, or at least before reading any further. This is because each exercise will shift your vibration and help you internalize what you are learning. That way, by the time you get to the final chapter, you'll be in the ideal energetic state to work your protection magic with sparkling success.

One more quick note: for this and the other visualizations in this book, just do your best. Don't worry about how "well" you are visualizing. Simply setting the intention to "see" something with your inner vision can cause powerful and positive shifts to occur beneath your conscious awareness, even if you don't seem to experience anything particularly vivid or impressive. The important thing is that you *do* the visualization exercises, not that you do them "right." Like anything else, the more you practice visualizing, the easier and more natural it will become. I promise you'll find your rhythm with it over time.

Violet Fire Visualization

Now back to the visualization at hand. This practice—the violet fire visualization—will help you transform fear into courage, peace, equanimity, or whatever mood and mindset will be most helpful for you at any given moment. It's an invaluable tool in protection magic. I predict you'll find yourself coming back to it again and again.

To begin, find a serene place where you won't be disturbed. Sit with your spine straight, in a comfortable (not rigid) way. If you'd like, you can light a purple candle, but this is not required. Take a few deep breaths, clear your mind, and relax your body. When you feel calm and centered, begin.

> *Close your eyes. Breathe naturally, but notice your breath. Watch yourself inhale and exhale, and feel the peace within the pause between each breath. Notice how simply bringing your awareness to your breathing naturally causes your breathing to deepen. [Pause to observe.]*
>
> *Now begin to notice the way it feels to be anchored into the earth with gravity. Can you feel your body pushing against the earth beneath you, holding you safely against the chair, the couch, or the floor? Imagine the depth of the*

earth beneath you. Get a sense of being anchored into the very core of the earth.

Now imagine the space above your head. Send your awareness above the roof, high into the sky, and beyond the earth's atmosphere. Imagine how vast our solar system is. And it's only a tiny part of our galaxy, which is just one of billions of galaxies. There is infinite space above you and around you. Realize that you are connected to this, too. Imagine that this infinite space is within your mind, your body, and your every cell. Sense it as potentiality: as the living light of all possibilities. You are connected to this light! Of course you are.

With your eyes still closed, call on the Goddess of the Moon. Ask her to manifest to the left of you, as if she is sitting on your left side, facing you. Feel a cool, receptive, loving presence on your left.

Call on the God of the Sun. Ask him to manifest to the right of you, as if he is sitting on your right side, facing you. Feel a bright, expansive, loving presence on your right.

Ask the Goddess and the God to direct their protective light toward you now. See and sense the Goddess projecting a beam of blue light toward you from the left at the same time that you see and sense the God projecting a beam of red light toward you from the right This is the brightest light you have ever seen. Much like the sun, it is blinding. As the two beams of light meet within your heart, they swirl into violet fire.

As you breathe in, see the violet fire at your heart becoming brighter and denser. As you breathe out, see it expand like a balloon.

Breathe in: the sphere of violet light becomes brighter.
Breathe out: the sphere of light expands even more.

Continue with this visualization until the violet sphere completely fills and encompasses you like a cozy bubble of light.

This violet fire is a transmuting flame. Anything you consciously send into it or offer up to it will transform into pure positivity and blessings.

Try it out. Take some deep breaths as you think of something you fear. Feel the fear as fully as you can as you breathe consciously and send the energy of the fear into the flames. As soon as the fear is consumed, it becomes bright, positive, protective energy. It becomes energy that will benefit you in exactly the way that is most needed.

The more fear you can feel, the more benefits you will accrue, so don't hold back. Continue to breathe as deeply and consciously as you can as you feel as much fear as possible. When you think you have finished feeling the fear, see if you can feel even more. Work with one fear or multiple fears. Sense the violet flame becoming brighter and more positive with every bit of fear you feel and offer up.

When this feels complete, realize that from now on, you can call on this violet fire anytime you wish. It is a gift from the Goddess and God, and it is a part of you.

Thank the Goddess of the Moon.

Thank the God of the Sun.

Take another deep, conscious breath and open your eyes.

In the future, when you want to work with the violet fire to clear and neutralize a feeling of fear (or any other challenging emotion), all you need to do is visualize the violet fire within and around you. Feel the fear as fully as you can as you breathe consciously and send the energy of the fear into the flames. The fire will transform the challenging qualities of the fear into precisely the positive and protective qualities that are most needed for you to thrive.

There's a good reason the violet fire exercise is the first one in this book. When your thoughts and feelings begin escalating in an uncomfortable way, and fighting against them only seems to make it worse, the violet fire is the most helpful exercise I know of to short-circuit this dynamic and bring you into a place of neutrality and calm—and this is exactly where you need to be for protection magic. So if your mind is worried, unsettled, or frenetic and you want to do a protection spell, now you have a practice that will help you clear the fear so you can begin.

If fear has been ruling you for a long time and you feel called to work with the violet fire every day for a while, you might like to fortify your efforts by wearing or carrying a sugilite, which is a crystal that is aligned with the energy of the violet fire. Once you obtain your sugilite, cleanse it and empower it by placing it in bright sunlight for a few minutes. If no sunlight is available, you can run cold water on it for a few minutes instead. Then hold it between your two palms in prayer pose, close your eyes, and charge the stone with the intention to help anchor your violet fire practice. Ask it to remind you to call on the violet fire if you experience fear, and to assist you in changing your inner momentum to one of positivity and courage. Feel that you are sending the energy of these thoughts and desires from your mind and body directly into the stone.

Hand It Over

Here's another essential habit for establishing equanimity that will serve you well not only in your protection magic but also throughout your lifetime. Old-timey metaphysical author and beloved affirmation pioneer Florence Scovel Shinn called it "casting the burden." I call it the "hand-it-over technique." No matter what you call it, the idea is to feel the fear or the worry or the terror, or whatever it is, and to realize you're holding onto it. It's as if you're carrying a heavy backpack or a giant suitcase filled with every frightening thing—known or unknown, conscious or unconscious—that you believe you have to conquer or surmount. You might even feel like you're carrying it in your heart or belly or on your shoulders.

Once you get a sense that you are indeed holding onto your fear or worry, and you feel the emotional and energetic weight of it, you let it go. But you don't just drop it anywhere. You *hand it over* to a divine helper or group of helpers whom you trust, knowing that they will know just where to take it and how to deal with it in order to support you in the best and most auspicious possible way.

When you get the hang of this technique, it not only helps you feel better immediately by relieving your present-moment concern, but also enlists divine support in clearing the road before you so you can move forward with ease and success in any given area of your life.

So let's give it a try. If you'd like, you can record this visualization as you did the last one, or you can just read it ahead of time to get an idea of what you'll be visualizing.

Begin by finding a quiet place where you won't be disturbed. Sit comfortably, close your eyes, and take some deep breaths. When your mind is clear and settled, begin.

> *Bring to mind something that worries or frightens you. It can be a big fear or a little fear. Whatever comes to mind first is best. Feel that fear or worry in your body, or envision it as a heavy bag you're carrying on your shoulders or back. This is the dense energy that results from hanging onto this fear. As you sense it, realize how tired you are of holding onto it. Imagine how freeing it would be to let it go.*
>
> *Now see or sense a divine being or group of beings in front of you. This could be an angel, a group of angels, or a particular divinity whom you revere, or it could be a beneficent presence or pillar of light. Now see or sense this being or group of beings holding out a large receptacle of light, such as a cauldron or bucket. As they do this, you know that they are asking you to hand over your burden of fear. And so you do.*
>
> *Feel the freedom of releasing this heavy weight into the receptacle. Sense the divine being or group of beings happily ascending to the heavenly realm with your fear, as if it were the lightest thing in the world. Know in your heart that they will take care of the situation in the way that is best for you and everyone concerned.*
>
> *Feel relieved and safe. Open your eyes.*

Much as with the violet fire visualization, once this becomes a habit, you will not need to close your eyes or stop what you're doing in order to hand over your fear. It can just be something you do as you go about your day.

In some cases, the fear or worry may seem to be stubborn and may present itself again and again on a loop in your mind. For example, this happened to me when my partner and I gave a thirty-day notice to our landlord before we had secured a new place to live. The worry that we would have nowhere to go kept showing up over and over again in my mind.

In a case like this, you might like to reinforce the hand-it-over technique with an affirmation, in order to systematically train your mind to let go of the worry and trust the Divine to take care of it. Naturally, you'll forget at times to inwardly repeat the affirmation, so anytime you notice that you've stopped, simply return your mind to the affirmation again and again. That way, you'll replace the old fearful thought loop with a new, more empowering and courageous one. (That's what I did, and it worked splendidly. We not only found a new place to live in plenty of time, but it was spectacular!)

My favorite affirmations for this purpose are inspired by Florence Scovel Shinn. Her affirmations often have a decidedly Christian slant, so I've adapted them to suit my personal non-sectarian preference. Work with one or both of these, or feel free to compose your own:

I cast the burden on the Divine within and I go free.

Infinite intelligence goes before me, making clear, easy, and successful my way.

Remember, choose one affirmation and stick with it until you don't need it anymore. Return to it again and again, so it's essentially on a loop in your inner monologue. Even though you will sometimes tune out while you are repeating your chosen affirmation, whenever you can, really consider the meaning of the words you are saying. Tap into the energy of the phrase, and feel the freedom of letting go of your worries and handing them over to the Divine.

Chapter 2

Align with the Divine

In the 1987 biographical documentary *A Hero's Journey*, professor Joseph Campbell said, "God is a metaphor for a mystery that absolutely transcends all human categories of thought…It's as simple as that."

Personally, I prefer the word *Divine* to *God*. I also sometimes use Source, Spirit, universe, infinite intelligence, or God/Goddess/All That Is. But it really doesn't matter what name you use. If you happen to like the word God, go with that. Or if you have another name you like that taps you into the idea of *that which transcends all levels of intellectual thought*, great.

Consider that *the fact of your existence* transcends all levels of rational thought. *What* you're made of and *how* it all works together can be explained and documented to some extent. The *why* of it, though, is not something our intellectual minds are even remotely able to grasp.

And while we can *ponder* infinity, comprehending the concept fully with our limited human minds is destined to perpetually elude us. Still, though, you are one with infinity. Time, eternity, the universe, the billions of galaxies, all of it: that's you, too. A single strand of DNA contains the whole blueprint within it. An acorn contains the potential for not just an oak tree but also a whole forest of oaks, and even more forests—countless forests—besides. You are like that strand of DNA and that acorn, containing the whole of the universe and infinity within you, and even within your every cell.

So when I counsel you to *align with the Divine* (which is the subject of this chapter), I am actually counseling you to realize what and who you already are, and to come into greater and greater resonance with this realization over time.

Still, even though you are indeed divinity in temporary human form, we must not forget the *temporary human form* part. So, yes, you're divine. And also, simultaneously…you're not. The level at which you are not divine is not a real level, but it seems real while you are here in this human body. So it has a relative reality. It is real in your perception. We can respect its reality when we know that it is not the whole story. Knowing you are made of stars, and that energy never dies, and that you are inextricably connected to All That Is, you are also, simultaneously, experiencing a finite human lifetime. You have a body that will perish. You have a name that labels you as *this and not that* (i.e., while you are Erin, you cannot also be Simon or Gail or Salvador). So on one level, you are not the Divine, while on a much truer level—an eternal level—you *are*.

You might think of it this way: Seen beyond the bounds of time, the acorn is countless forests of oak trees. Seen within the bounds of time, it is only an acorn. The latter is true for a brief, passing moment. The former is true for eternity. But both are true.

Of course, most of your everyday human experience is perceived through the lens of being just an acorn. As long as you are having this human experience, you are buying into and perpetuating this story of being limited, separate, small, and…*not infinite*. But one of the secrets to working successful magic—and this is especially helpful in protection magic—is remembering your true, unlimited nature in order to positively affect your limited human experience. And that's what we call *aligning with the Divine.*

Thanks to the previous chapter, you've already begun aligning with the Divine. When you feel worry or fear within your little acorn self and then release it with trust to the forest of wise old oaks, it is a process of releasing your hold on the concept of the little you and opening up to the power that lies outside of the little you. As you may have noticed, when you do this, you can sense that even though the power lies outside of the little you, it is not separate from you, because you are actually so much more than the little you. You are inextricably woven into the web of light that is everything: infinity, divinity, and that which transcends all levels of rational thought. God, if you like. Or Goddess. You get the picture.

In this chapter, you'll continue this great work of aligning with the Divine in order to begin resonating with a naturally protective frequency: a vibration that will serve as the perfect canvas for successful protection magic while simultaneously acting as a protective force field in its own right.

Get Your House in Order

Believe it or not, anytime you learn a new kind of magic or refine your understanding of metaphysical principles of any variety, cleaning your house will help. So will clearing clutter and organizing.

This is because real magic starts with our relationship to the physical world. From there, we are reminded that everything is connected: form and spirit, seen and unseen, known and unknown. So getting your home in order gets your spirit in order. Clearing away clutter, cobwebs, and dust clears the way for your intentions and desired life conditions to manifest easily, rapidly, and in the most auspicious possible ways.

Even if you're a pretty neat person, clutter and dust will still accumulate in drawers, crannies, and corners. So in just a moment, I'm going to ask you to put this book down so you can clean your house. First, be sure to let go of anything you no longer need by donating it to a thrift store or food bank, recycling it, or giving it away to someone who genuinely wants it and could really use it. Then you can move on to organizing shelves, drawers, closets, cupboards, and desks.

Is there someone from your past who causes you to feel unsafe in any way, such as an ex who turned into a stalker or anyone whose name you've asked a judge to put on a restraining order? Or even just an ex you never want to see or talk to ever again? If so, make sure you don't have any of their stuff in your house, and also get rid of any photos of them, items you once co-owned with them, and gifts you received from them. This is because these objects resonate with this person's frequency.

So you might say that holding on to the objects is like letting this person keep your house key: it makes it easier for them to wedge their way into your energetic space.

Feel free to play music while you clean. Music helps move stuck energy while bringing new, harmonious energetic patterns into your space. Classical and New Age music are particularly helpful for these aims. But for deep clutter clearing, play any music that resonates with your current mood in order to help unstick the emotions held in place by the stuff you're releasing. (Sad music can help you release sad emotions, angry music can help you release angry emotions, and so on.) You can also burn incense or diffuse essential oil to further shift the vibration in a positive way, if you don't have any children, partners, or animals who are sensitive to it.

Don't worry if clearing all your clutter seems too daunting right now. If you can clear all of it before moving on to the next section of the book, great! If not, just get started and make a plan to continue. (For example, you might commit to clearing for fifteen minutes a day five days a week, or two hours once per week, etc. Whatever you can reasonably commit to, put it in your calendar and stick to it.)

Clean and clear with focus and intention, but don't feel that you need to rush through this. You came here to learn protection magic, and the more vibrantly clean and organized you can get your home, the more resonant you will be with the energy I want you to call in for this stage in your journey.

So now's the time: close the book and clean.

Basic Home Protection Ritual

Once your house is clean and you've also cleared any clutter from your porch, yard, and other outdoor areas, it's time for a basic home protection ritual.

First, put a few drops of spearmint essential oil in a bucket and fill it with warm water. Using a clean rag, wash first the inside and then the outside of your front door. Repeat this process (with a fresh bucket of water) for any additional doors to the outside. If any of them are made of glass or contain glass windows, use a mixture of one part white vinegar to three parts water to wash the glass, using a paper towel instead of a rag.

Now that your doors are clean, peel a clove of garlic and slice it in half. Touch the outside of your front door with the cut side of the garlic to lightly anoint it with the juice. As you do this, feel that you are filling the entire door and threshold with a blinding white light of positivity through which no negativity or ill will may enter. Repeat with any additional doors to the outside. Finish by calling on the Divine in a way that feels powerful to you to seal your home in a sphere of positive and protective light. (Then release the garlic to the earth or a compost bin.)

Can you feel the vibrational shift in your home? After you've cleaned, cleared, and performed a protective ritual, you're likely to find that your home feels safer, brighter, and more positive than it did before. This, in turn, will naturally affect the way you feel about yourself and your life.

This would be a good time to honestly assess your home's degree of physical security. Do all the doors to the outside lock securely, and do you keep them locked on a regular basis? Are your valuables reasonably secure, and do you have sufficient insurance? Are your fire and carbon monoxide alarms working properly? Would it make sense to install a deadbolt, security camera, or alarm system? Remember, being careful is not the same thing as letting your fear rule you. Actually, it's a way of letting your fear *serve* you by letting it spur you to take positive action. And as I said in the introduction, it's always a good idea to work on both the physical and energetic levels at once, so they can reinforce each other.

A Fierce Aura

Your aura is your personal energy field: the body of light that underlies your physicality, weaving together and interacting with your mind, body, and spirit. *Fierce* is an apt adjective to describe the quality of energy you want to emanate for our present purposes. It's a proactive word: it acts instead of retreats, and it shines like white fire. In this empowering meditation, you'll be aligning with divine energy to cultivate an aura of fierceness.

This is a variation of a type of meditation practice I call *magical hygiene,* which is something I recommend doing every day. Before you begin, you can either record yourself speaking these words or commit the steps to memory.

If you'd like, you can light a white candle and burn frankincense, sandalwood, or cedar incense (or diffuse the essential oil) while you meditate. While these tools may assist you in focusing your mind and entering a meditative state, neither is required.

Magical Hygiene Meditation

Find someplace quiet and comfortable where you won't be disturbed. Sit with your spine straight, in a comfortable (not rigid) way. Then begin.

Close your eyes. Breathe in deeply. Hold for a count of three. Breathe out and hold for a count of three. Repeat two more times. Now allow your breathing to be natural, but continue to observe it. Notice as you breathe in, notice as you breathe out, and notice the pause between the breaths. If your mind wanders, no problem: simply bring it back to the breath. As you do this, you'll notice that your mindfulness naturally expands to include your body. If you notice any tension in your body, send energy to it as you breathe in, and imagine that you are creating space there. As you breathe out, feel that you are letting the tension go. Continue to place your attention on your breath until you feel sufficiently centered and calm.

Now call on the Divine in a way that feels powerful for you. Ask divine energy to completely clear you of any and all stuck or challenging energy. Imagine, feel, or sense a glowing vacuum tube of blinding white light moving through your body and aura, removing any heaviness, tension, fear, or challenging energy of any kind.

Next, ask the Divine to completely fill and surround you with golden white light. See, feel, or sense your body transforming into light. Imagine this light expanding into a sphere around you, so you are completely filled with and cocooned in light. With the help of the Divine, set the intention that within this sphere, only love remains, and through this sphere, only love may enter.

Breathe in light and breathe out light. Imagine the sphere of light within and around you becoming brighter and more positive as you breathe. Feel and sense that you are radiating such fierce positivity that the energy in the room is becoming clearer and more positive just because you are sitting in it.

Continue to sense yourself as light as you bring your attention to the feeling of being anchored into the earth beneath you. Feel gravity pulling you down in the most natural and comforting way. Now, from your tailbone, imagine you are sending a taproot of light down into Mother Earth. This root naturally goes straight down, further and further, until it reaches the core of the earth. You can imagine the core of the earth as a golden-white sphere, like a miniature sun in the center of the planet. As your root of light enters this sphere of light, it's like plugging a cord into an outlet: it begins to recharge you with this beautiful, grounded energy at the center of the earth. This earth light moves up your root steadily and swiftly until it enters your tailbone.

Feel your legs, hips, and pelvis illuminate and relax with this influx of golden-white earth energy. Feel your lower belly, upper belly, inner organs, and back illuminate and relax. Feel this warm, expansive energy moving into your heart and chest, your lungs, your upper back. Feel it relaxing your shoulders, moving down through your arms and into your hands. Sense it filling your upper chest and throat and relaxing your neck. Sense your entire brain being massaged with golden-white earth energy. Feel it relax your face, your ears, and your scalp.

Now, from the crown of your head, send a trunk of light up into the sky. See the light growing upward steadily. Imagine it moving up, up, up, out of the earth's atmosphere, into space, and into a diamond-white realm that symbolizes infinity. Just as you plugged your energy field into the earth, now imagine you are plugging your personal energy field into this infinite diamond-white light. Realize that infinity is familiar to you because it is your true identity, and watch as this diamond-white light naturally begins to move down the trunk of light and into the crown of your head.

Now the diamond-white light of infinity is mixing with the golden-white light of the earth. It's massaging your scalp, filling your brain, and relaxing your face. It's moving down into your throat, illuminating your neck, and loosening any tension in your shoulders and upper back. It's filling your heart and lungs and moving down your arms and into your hands. This diamond light continues down into your upper belly, inner organs, and back. It moves into your lower belly, sex organs, and tailbone. It fills your legs and your feet.

Now you are a sphere of light, connected to both the earth and the cosmos. Feel your power and your natural, inexhaustible sources of energy and inspiration coming to you from both above and below. Realize that you are the master of your domain. With your intuition dialed into both the earth and the cosmos, you can easily tune in to what feels right to you and what doesn't, and you can also access clear and loving divine guidance about how to speak your truth, assert your boundaries, and act on your inner nudges.

Your aura is so fierce and so bright that wherever you go, you will spread positive energy. Because you will be emanating this positivity so strongly, you will not be open to negativity, and negativity will naturally avoid you.

> *Take some more deep, conscious breaths, feeling that you are creating even more space within your every cell for vibrant positivity to radiate and flow.*
>
> *Feel gratitude to the earth. Feel gratitude to the cosmos. Feel gratitude for being a channel of pure positivity and love. Then open your eyes.*

How do you feel? You're feeling pretty different than you did before, I'd wager. Even if you don't notice anything particularly dramatic right away, I'm willing to bet you'll notice yourself interacting with the world differently throughout the remainder of the day.

Even though performing a magical hygiene meditation like this one affects your personal energy field instantly, it also has cumulative benefits. When you repeat such a meditation daily, your personal energy field (and, consequently, the way you feel in your body and the world) changes profoundly over time. Feeling fiercely positive becomes your default setting, the rule rather than the exception. And when you notice this is not the case, you can instinctively bring yourself back into an energetically harmonious state.

That's why, starting now, I'd like for you to perform this meditation, or one like it, daily. I say "one like it" because you'll likely begin to make it your own over time. As long as you're clearing and shielding your energy, and also connecting your energy field to the golden light at the core of the earth and the diamond light of infinity, you're good. Those are the primary dynamics you want to include. In addition to priming your mind, body, and spirit for successful protection magic, a daily magical hygiene practice will bring profound, lifelong benefits. These benefits include, but are not limited to, the following:

- Greater confidence
- Energy and enthusiasm
- Magnetic attractiveness
- Crystal-clear intuition
- Increased personal power
- Greater ease in manifesting your desires
- Enhanced physical and emotional well-being

If you happen to skip a day, or even if your magical hygiene practice drops off for a week or a month, all is not lost. Without judging or berating yourself, just start up again. Then repeat the next day, and the next. As with any habit you want to develop, the secret is showing up as much as you can, again and again, until it becomes second nature.

Chapter 3

Angelic Forces

You may have some assumptions about angels. You may think they're cutesy or twee or always floating around smiling and wearing lace gowns. You may think they are exclusive to the big three monotheistic faiths. Or, like some magical practitioners I know, you may believe none of these things about angels, but rather that they are so powerful that you shouldn't mess around with them unless circumstances are dire.

As we begin this chapter, if you happen to hold any of these assumptions (or any other ones), I'm requesting that you set them aside. At the end of this chapter, if you decide you'd like to pick them back up again, you certainly may. All I ask is that you clear your mind of them for the moment so I can acquaint you with these protection magic superheroes.

The word *angel* comes from *angelos*, which is a Greek translation of a Hebrew word meaning "messenger." A messenger is a go-between: someone who facilitates communication between two beings who are physically separate. While we are not actually separate from infinite intelligence, we *are* temporarily showing up in finite human form. So we *seem* to be separate. While we are in this perceived state of separation, it is impossible for our minds to fully grasp or contain infinity (also known as divinity, also known as God/Goddess/All That Is). We can sense it, and we can connect with it, but we need some sort of conceptual or symbolic mediation—some sort of *messenger*—in order to do so.

One metaphor I find helpful when describing angels is a rainbow. If you think of the Divine as pure sunlight, you can think of angels as the colors of the rainbow that create the spectrum of light we can see with our human eyes. When sunlight bends through a prism or raindrops, we can see these colors arrayed, and they have meaning for us in the finite world that appears before us: red is a strawberry, yellow is a daffodil, blue is the sky. In truth, it's still pure white light. But to us, it has become more relatable. We can see and perceive the many ways it appears to us while we are in this human form on earth. It's as if the rainbow is a messenger of the light: it shows us the different aspects of the light that are otherwise invisible to us or beneath our conscious awareness.

When we imagine angels to have human faces and forms, it's not because they actually do; it's because we are conceptualizing them, i.e., translating their essence into symbols we can understand and relate to. More accurately (but still speaking metaphorically), angels are like rays or laser beams of living divine intelligence. Because we are also a part of divine intelligence, we can invoke and benefit from these currents of divinity. That's what it means to call on angels.

Why is calling on angels so vital to protection magic? Because when you tap into angelic energy, wisdom, and guidance, you lock into pure positivity: you align with whatever is for your truest and most authentic good. You might say this is the opposite of fear and worry, because it reminds you that you are connected to something much bigger and more powerful than your limited human brain and body. Even if you can't see the big picture with your little human eyes, and even if you can't perfectly orchestrate every detail of your life experience, you remember that you are connected to something that can: you're one with the omnipotent intelligence that created you, and you're able to invoke and interweave this intelligence into every aspect of your life.

Angels are accessible to everyone. As a divine child, it is your birthright to work with them. If you ask an angel for assistance, you will always receive it. That is, you will always receive it if you also choose to allow it. *Allowing* means energetically releasing the problem enough to allow angelic assistance to flow in. For example, if you ask someone to drive your car but then refuse to get out of the driver's seat, you've asked for assistance, but you're not actually allowing yourself to receive it. Of course, allowing angels to help you isn't as straightforward as literally getting out of the driver's seat. It could be more like consciously relaxing your body, taking a deep breath, or simply choosing to trust that the divine help you've requested is actually on its way. This allowing part is important because the angels always respect our free will. Even if we verbally request their assistance, if they can energetically sense that we are not willing to allow them to help us, they won't help us. The good news is that allowing angelic assistance is a skill: as with any skill, with practice, it becomes second nature.

Next you'll meet four archangels who are particularly helpful for protection magic. While you may want to work with additional archangels at some point, if you cultivate a working relationship with these four, you'll have access to all the angelic protection you need.

Archangel Michael

Think of the sunlight at noon when there's not a cloud in the sky. Perhaps you're on a tropical beach, in a desert, or at a particularly high elevation: someplace where the sun seems to be even more blindingly bright than usual. Now imagine the sun descending so it's shining before you. In your mind's eye, step into the center of that sun. Feel it burning away all negativity and cocooning you in the most powerful possible energetic protection. That's the best way I can describe Archangel Michael's energy: purely positive, fiercely protective fire.

I name Michael first because in my experience, he is the most helpful archangel for protection magic. When you call on him, whether you do so silently or aloud, he arrives instantly. And provided you allow his assistance, he will never fail to protect you from both inner and outer dangers.

For example, when I lived in Venice Beach in Los Angeles, I entered my home through an alley. One day as I was walking home from the grocery store toward my gate, the alley was empty except for a lone man who was yelling loudly and hitting cars and fences with his fists. Although I was already in his line of sight, I instantly ducked behind some cars and called on Archangel Michael. While I was essentially cornered, with nowhere to go to avoid crossing paths with this man, a police car happened to cruise by…in the alley! This wasn't something I had ever witnessed, and it happened immediately after I requested Michael's help. While the police officer had his eyes on the man, I was able to easily slip by and safely enter the gate behind my apartment complex. (I'm sure it's no coincidence that the Catholic Church named Archangel Michael the patron saint of law enforcement officers.)

Another time, I was staying in a hotel that was part of a historic Masonic lodge that I felt was particularly haunted. While this haunted feeling was intriguing and otherworldly during waking hours, once the lights were out, I felt unsettled in a way I rarely do. I felt spirits hanging around me, and not beneficent ones. Instead of going into pure panic mode (which didn't feel like it would be too hard to do), I chose to call on Archangel Michael to surround me in a sphere of protective light. This settled my mind and spirit and helped me feel safe. Admittedly, I still didn't get the best night's sleep, but I sure felt better than I otherwise would have, and I believe I avoided being negatively affected by the unquiet spirits I sensed in that space.

Both of these incidents illustrate the way Michael shows up immediately when we call on him, in order to provide powerful protection in both the seen and unseen worlds.

Archangel Raphael

Bring to mind the last time you were up early enough to go outside and watch the sunrise. I'm sure you'll agree that when the sun peeks over the horizon, a rare and exquisite feeling dawns within you. It's as if the loving, living presence of the whole sky is smiling at you, surrounding you, and suffusing your heart. There's a silent awareness that is almost palpable, and it's filled with intelligence. You make contact with the vast, open space of consciousness that is who you really are. You feel infinite doors of possibility opening for you. You may even get the sense that it's easy to bring your body and mind into perfect health, because wellness is your natural state. That's the essence of Archangel Raphael.

Archangel Raphael supports healing on all levels, and he helps us keep our heart open so we can consistently connect with the energy of love. When you work with Archangel Raphael regularly, he helps you maintain a harmonious frequency that naturally helps prevent negativity from entering your personal space. Archangel Raphael also works together with Archangel Michael to energetically clear your body, mind, aura, and physical space, and to shield and protect you from all forms of harm.

If I feel tired, in pain, depressed, or under the weather, I call on Archangel Raphael to help me heal and to intuit what will help me feel better and thrive. This, in turn, boosts my energetic vibrancy and my aura's natural protective properties. Raphael is also the angel I call on whenever I want to send healing energy to another person. Even though I've worked with Raphael for years, it still surprises me how quickly his support can arrive.

Archangel Chamuel

Have you ever shut someone out of your life because your relationship with them was unhealthy, toxic, codependent, or otherwise depleting in some way? If so, you probably learned that even though it can be painful to say no to a relationship that is out of alignment with integrity, it's also one of the most loving things you can do—and not just for yourself! Ultimately, everyone benefits when you speak and enforce your truth about what you are no longer willing to allow into your life. This is as true for situations (such as jobs, commitments, and living arrangements) as it is for people.

Archangel Chamuel helps us to be honest with ourselves about our needs, and to speak up about those needs in our relationships. While his loving, heart-opening aspects are often noted over his ability to help us set strong and healthy boundaries, these two spheres of angelic support go hand in hand. When it comes to protection magic, Archangel Chamuel will help you recognize the difference between people and situations that support you and those that tear you down or drain you.

Of course, close relationships always involve disagreements, and no job or living situation is always perfect. But there's a difference between being challenged in a healthy way and being challenged in a way that is out of alignment with what is best for you. Chamuel can help you to tell the difference and to stand your ground when it comes to letting go of what you no longer want in your life.

In much the same way that a well-secured home can help you let down your guard and be fully yourself, setting strong energetic and emotional boundaries can actually help you open your heart to life and loved ones *more*, not less. So you can see why strong love and strong boundaries are inextricably intertwined, and why it makes sense that Chamuel helps us out with both.

I first began working with Archangel Chamuel when I had to set a boundary with a close female relative. While I had tried my best, I finally realized that continuing a relationship with her just wasn't going to work. It was a painful time in my life, and even though I was able to enforce the boundary physically, it wasn't as easy for me to separate from this relative energetically. Archangel Chamuel showed up in my meditations around this time. His sweet, loving presence, combined with his fierce "thou shall not pass" vibe, was just the balm I needed to heal from this emotional wound and challenging energetic dynamic.

Archangel Zaphkiel

Even though modern life can often feel frenetic, it's likely that you have experienced rare, precious moments in your life when you got in touch with a sense of profound silence, serenity, and space. Perhaps during meditation, while walking outside in nature, or while soaking in a hot bath. This deep inner quiet describes the essence of Zaphkiel. As an angel of Saturn (the planet of limits and boundaries), she helps us to let go of what doesn't serve us and to proactively dissolve and destroy patterns, relationships, and situations that it would benefit us to release.

Sometimes we need to invoke protection not from outer dangers but rather from inner patterns of thought and feeling, such as habits of worry, anxiety, and self-criticism. When this is the case, Zaphkiel can help. When you notice your mind spiraling into an unhelpful monologue again and again, or when a fearful feeling seems to be your default setting, calling on Zaphkiel (again and again if necessary) can help erase these inner dangers and fill you with a sense of stillness, openness, and quiet.

Zaphkiel also helps when we feel that we've been cursed in some way, or that we've picked up an energy or entity we don't want in our aura, or when we are in a relationship pattern that we want to let go of for good. She does this by cutting the cords, banishing the energy, or destroying the pattern that has been holding us back (or all of the above).

When my mind becomes an uncomfortable place to be because of a pattern of worry, fear, or self-criticism, I love to call on Archangel Zaphkiel. Her strong, silent presence instantly takes over, replacing my frenetic thought patterns with stillness and calm. Even if I need to call on her multiple times in response to a particularly stubborn cycle of thought, each time I call on her, the thought pattern fades more and more, until Zaphkiel's serenity reigns supreme.

Angelic Tune-In Ritual

Now it's time to meet these four archangels. Even if you're already familiar with one or more of them, this ritual will help you attune with their energy for the purpose of protection magic.

If you don't already know the cardinal directions in your space, use a compass to determine east, south, west, and north. (There should be a compass in the utilities section of your smartphone.)

Gather these items:

- 1 royal blue candle
- 1 vibrant green candle (such as kelly green, grass green, apple green, jade green, or emerald green)
- 1 red candle
- 1 black candle
- A lighter or matches

Any type of candle will do, but it's best if they're all the same shape and size. Use candleholders if necessary.

Find someplace clean and quiet where you won't be disturbed. Place your candles on the floor around you: green to the east, blue to the south, black to the west, and red to the north. Be sure to place them safely, so nothing will catch fire when they are lit, including you. Also be sure there are no small children or animals in the room.

Sit comfortably in the center of the candles while facing east. Sit with your spine straight, in a comfortable, relaxed way. You can sit on the floor, a cushion, or a chair, whatever you prefer.

Close your eyes and take some deep breaths. Then allow your breathing to be natural, but continue to observe it. If your mind wanders, don't worry: just bring it back to the breath without judgment. Stay with this conscious breathing practice until your mind is clear and calm and your body feels relaxed and open.

Feel your weight on the chair, cushion, or floor, anchoring you into the earth. Let this feeling remind you of the energetic aliveness of your body, and begin to feel and sense your body as made up of golden-white light. Imagine anchoring your energy into the earth from your tailbone and legs. Send a taproot or pillar of light deep into the center of the earth, and connect with the golden-white magnetic energy at the earth's core. Feel this earth energy connecting with and replenishing your personal energy. Now send a pillar or trunk of light from the crown of your head up to the very center of the sun. Anchor your energy field into the sun, and feel its golden-white light connect with and replenish your personal light and move all the way down to the core of the earth. Feel and sense this light expanding now so you are contained within a large pillar of light connecting the center of the earth to the center of the sun.

Open your eyes. Light the green candle in front of you. Close your eyes again and say:

Archangel Raphael, I call on you.

Feel, imagine, and sense the pillar of light that contains, fills, and surrounds you becoming a vibrant emerald green. Imagine this light connecting all the way to the core of the earth and the center of the sun. Sense Archangel Raphael's loving and balancing energy suffuse you. Feel it healing you and opening your heart. When this feels complete, open your eyes.

Turn so you are facing south. Light the blue candle. Close your eyes and say:

Archangel Michael, I call on you.

Feel, imagine, and sense the pillar of light becoming a bright royal blue, anchoring you into the center of earth and the center of the sun. Breathe this royal blue light in and out as you sense Archangel Michael's bright, protective energy bolstering you and surrounding you in radiant positivity in which no negativity can remain and through which no negativity can penetrate. When you're ready, open your eyes.

Turn so you are facing west. Light the black candle. Close your eyes and say:

Archangel Zaphkiel, I call on you.

Feel, imagine, and sense the pillar of light becoming a radiant, absorbent black color that cocoons you in beautiful serenity and silence all the way from the center of the earth to the center of the sun. Feel this black ray of light neutralizing all fear, worry, and unhelpful patterns of thought, energy, and emotion. Feel and sense it filling you with the strength and steadiness you need in order to let go of everything that no longer serves you, whether it arises from within you or outside of you. Then open your eyes.

Turn so you are facing north. Light the red candle. Close your eyes and say:

Archangel Chamuel, I call on you.

Sense the pillar of light becoming ruby red. Feel the strength of this color as it anchors you into the center of the earth and the center of the sun. Feel this pillar of red light bolstering your connection to your courage and your truth. Sense it anchoring you in your power, and feel the thrill of embodying your power. Allow this red light to infuse your entire body and aura, and notice how it transforms stuck energy into enthusiasm, energy, and movement. Open your eyes.

Face east once again. Sense the steadfast presence of these angels around you, and know that you can call on them for support whenever you need to. Feel the joy of knowing you are lovingly supported in this way.

Still feeling this gratitude, say:

Archangel Raphael, thank you.

Then blow out the green candle.
Face north. Say:

Archangel Chamuel, thank you.

Blow out the red candle.
Face west. Say:

Archangel Zaphkiel, thank you.

Blow out the black candle.
Face south. Say:

Archangel Michael, thank you.

Blow out the blue candle.
Face east. Place your hands on your heart and say:

Thank you, thank you, thank you. Blessed be. And so it is.

Now have a little something to eat to help ground your energy, like a cookie or a granola bar.

Now that you're familiar with these angels and have magically attuned yourself to their presence, you can call on any of them at any time. To do so, simply say, silently or aloud, "Archangel _____, I call on you." Then ask for or envision the type of support you need. Relax and trust as much as you can so that you will be in a receptive state to allow the help you have requested to arrive.

If you'd like, you can light a candle before you invoke the support of a particular angel. You can use the candles you've just employed in the ritual (green for Raphael, blue for Michael, black for Zaphkiel, and red for Chamuel). In the future, when those candles have burned down, you can replace them with other candles of the same color or another color that is in alignment with the angel you're invoking. The following colors are associated with these four archangels:

Raphael: Green, pink, or gold

Michael: Blue, white, or gold

Zaphkiel: Black, gray, or lilac

Chamuel: Red or pink

I believe you'll find working with angels to be practical, reliable, and uplifting. Additionally, you'll discover that they're both universally accessible and vastly powerful (and certainly not cutesy).

Chapter 4

Basic Protection Techniques

Here's a definition for you: *magic is a way of shaping, directing, and channeling invisible forces in order to create the conditions you desire.*

In this chapter, you'll learn about four primary magical dynamics that will help you in protection magic. You'll find it much easier to understand these dynamics if you begin by thinking of yourself not as merely a human body—beginning and ending with your bones, muscles, organs, and skin—but rather as a sphere of energy: an aura. Of course you have a body. But that body is animated by, filled with, and surrounded by energy. When working magic, it is most useful to conceive of yourself as this energetic being: a sphere or bubble of consciousness and light.

This awareness of yourself as a glowing ball of energy shouldn't be totally new to you. At the very least, by working with the exercises in the previous chapters, you've already played with this concept a little. Let's refresh this awareness now.

In just a moment, I want you to close your eyes and feel the energetic aliveness of your body. Feel your weight on the earth and the air moving in and out of your lungs. Inwardly see or sense your aliveness as conscious, spiritual light. Imagine that the energy that fills and animates you is as blindingly bright as the sun. Now, as you breathe, feel how this light extends outward all around you. Do your best to hold an image of your body as a ball of light, containing you, protecting you, and defining where you end and the rest of the world begins. This light extends above your head, below your feet, and around you equally in all directions. Okay, ready? Go.

Were you able to get in touch with this inner vision of yourself as a glowing ball of energy? Try it again if necessary and go deeper. But don't worry if you aren't able to powerfully connect with this image just yet. Just setting the intention to surround yourself in light is enough. The more often you work with this visualization, the clearer it will become.

One more note before we get into specifics: you don't need any magical tools or ingredients for the following protection techniques. However, there are certain crystals, botanicals, and talismanic symbols that can be employed to amplify and support these practices in various ways. You'll learn more about such items in the next chapter. For now, we'll focus on the techniques themselves.

Radiate

You've probably had the experience of going out into the world—even somewhere as seemingly innocuous as a supermarket or bank—and then somehow managing to soak up negative, stressful, or unhappy energy, so that you left feeling much worse than when you arrived. Maybe there was an interaction that caused it, or maybe the undesirable energy was just hanging around in the atmosphere, with no clear origin, waiting to be absorbed. Either way, this dynamic can be prevented when you draw upon your ability to consciously radiate energy outward.

When you are open to any old energy floating around, you are like a sponge. When, on the other hand, you are consciously radiating positive energy, you reverse the direction in which that energy is flowing. When you are a ball of radiant positivity, energy is shining out of you in such abundance that it's unlikely that any energy that doesn't match that is going to flow in. In this way, you affect your environment rather than allowing your environment to affect you.

Now, it may seem like this would drain you. Wouldn't you end up feeling sort of used up if you went around shining positive light all the time? Well, if you believed you had to generate all that positivity from some sort of performance—like cheesy compliments, fake smiles, and clever small talk—then, yes, you would feel drained. But if the positivity you're radiating is authentic, and not based on how you're *acting* but on how you're *being*, then nope! Radiating means being a channel of light rather than a generator of it. When you radiate correctly, your energy will be plugged into the core of the earth and the infinite light of the cosmos, so the more you shine, the more positivity you will feel.

And, of course, it's a reliable magical law that *what you send out comes back to you multiplied.* So positive energy will boomerang back to you in spades.

Whenever you do your magical hygiene meditation (as described at the end of chapter 2), you are connecting with the energy at the core of the earth as well as the energy of the infinite cosmos. In this way, you set yourself up to radiate positivity in an authentic, sustainable way. So before you enter a grocery store, a bank, a dreaded family gathering, an awkward work party, or whatever it is, you can set the intention to radiate positivity, and you can call on angels or divine energy to help you do that. Then simply bring to mind—visualize, imagine, or sense—this energetic dynamic at work. Again, this has nothing to do with how you outwardly act. You can be silent and blank-faced or chatty and smiley, whatever feels right. The important thing is what is happening in the invisible realm: your steadfast emanation of positive, divine power, anchored in the earth and continually nourished by the infinite light of the cosmos. You are like a miniature sun lighting up the room with your aura of positivity and peace.

It's a good idea to get in the habit of radiating positivity when you go out in the world. Over time, it will become your default setting, so you'll naturally be cocooned in positivity wherever you go, and you'll share that vibration with the people and places in your personal orbit. Will you sometimes be in a bad mood? Sure! We all go through fluctuations. This isn't about being a Pollyanna; it's about getting in the habit of being a divine channel rather than a human sponge. We're talking about a predominant energetic pattern, not a perpetual mood.

Shield

Shielding your energy means surrounding yourself in a sphere of divine energy and love, through which no negativity may enter or dwell. You can also shield other people, vehicles, and spaces with such energy. Once again, your magical hygiene meditation (from chapter 2) has prepared you for this practice, as shielding is conveniently built into it.

Shielding is similar to radiating but also different. While radiating is a way of channeling and spreading light, shielding is a way of setting a boundary in order to determine what you do and do not want to enter your space.

An energetic shield is not like an armored vehicle that keeps its passengers hidden away and walled off from the outside world. You can think of it instead as porous: as something that allows you to see and be seen, as well as connect deeply and meaningfully with others, while also alerting you to energies that don't match your positive intentions for yourself, so you can shift them, say no to them, or simply choose to avoid them.

A Course in Miracles teaches that everything is either love or a call for love. An energetic shield helps keep you grounded in and surrounded by love, so if you observe actions or situations that seem to be out of alignment with love, you can perceive the cry for love that is actually behind them. Seeing the world through eyes of love is actually protective, because it transforms not only the way you interact with the world but also the way the world interacts with you.

Your daily magical hygiene meditation includes a shielding practice. Still, there may be times when you'd like to add an additional shield. For example, I once felt compelled to attend a wedding celebration that promised to be filled with family drama, which I was not looking forward to dealing with. In the car on the way to the event, a beloved family member and I called on the Divine to shield us with a sphere of pink light. We envisioned ourselves in a bubble of sweet, soft energy, and we set the intention that while we might observe weirdness happening around us, we wouldn't get caught up in it or absorb any unsettling vibes. The shield worked like a charm.

Why did we choose pink? Well, my family member actually chose the color, but I agreed that it felt right. You can do the same by choosing a shield in a color that feels empowering to you for the situation at hand. Or, if you like, you can use the following correspondences as a general guide:

- **White light:** All-purpose positivity and protection, cosmic energy, divine energy
- **Golden-white light:** Balancing and harmonizing positivity and protection, earth energy, aligned with all angels and the angelic realm
- **Black:** Absorbent; helps neutralize and dissolve stress, worry, frenetic energy, and all forms of negativity
- **Brown:** Grounding, calming, relaxing
- **Pink:** Loving, positive, sweet, aligned with the feminine aspect of Archangel Chamuel
- **Violet:** Transmuting/transforming light
- **Lilac:** Inner silence and serenity, helpful for releasing negative thought patterns, aligned with Archangel Zaphkiel
- **Royal blue:** Strong positivity and protection, aligned with Archangel Michael
- **Sky blue:** Empowers self-expression

- **Teal:** Stress-relieving, strengthens immunity
- **Green:** Holistic wellness, openheartedness, aligned with Archangel Raphael
- **Yellow:** Personal power, grounding
- **Orange:** Courage, harmony, strength
- **Red:** Success, prosperity, strength, aligned with Archangel Chamuel
- **Magenta or rose gold:** Body positivity, goddess energy, self-love and self-approval

Keep in mind that when you visualize light, no matter what color you're visualizing, it helps to imagine it shining with the blinding brightness of the sun.

Deflect

When you were a kid and someone called you a name, did you ever say this: "I'm rubber, you're glue, whatever you say bounces off of me and sticks to you." If so, you were performing a little deflection magic. This is a dynamic that involves sending energy straight back to where it came from. While cursing or hexing someone isn't something I generally recommend, for very good karmic reasons, you can certainly send negative energy back to its source without your karma suffering a bit.

Deflecting is a common feng shui tactic when it comes to problematic neighbors. Regardless of the challenging behavior—whether it's noise, rudeness, or anything else—feng shui wisdom recommends positioning a mirror so that the reflective side is facing your neighbor's place. Then you set the intention that any and all energy that comes your way from the general direction of your neighbors (whether it's good, bad, or anywhere in between) will bounce straight back to them. For example, if they're loud, their loudness will annoy them instead of you, and they will naturally want to stop making so much noise, or for some other reason you just won't seem to notice it as much. (You'll find more detailed instructions for working with mirrors in the next chapter.)

But you don't need a mirror in order to deflect. For example, when I lived in Los Angeles, I constantly felt vulnerable when I went out in the world. Being from a small town, I wasn't accustomed to all the glances, stares, and comments I constantly seemed to be receiving from strangers. When I wanted to shut it all out, I would envision a mirrored sphere around myself. I set the intention that anyone looking my direction wouldn't see me, but instead would see themselves reflected back to them. While I believe this effect was more figurative than literal, the mirrored sphere visualization was effective at helping me feel safely removed from the emotional and energetic orbits of any and all strangers and passersby. You can use a similar visualization anytime you want to deflect energy back to its source.

Mudras, or hand gestures, can also be helpful for deflecting energy. You know when someone flashes their palm in a "talk to the hand" gesture? That's a form of conversational deflection. You can do the same on an energetic level, without ever having to utter an unkind word. Let's say you're in a meeting at work and you feel negative vibes emanating from a coworker. Subtly, under the table, you could hold up your hand and imagine your hand is acting like a mirror, instantly and completely sending all their energy straight back to them.

When I was a little girl, an Italian relative of mine taught me a similar practice to ward off the evil eye, a sort of curse believed to be dispensed with a glower or glare. "If you think someone is giving you the evil eye," he said, "do this." Then he showed me the "sign of the horns," a gesture that, incidentally, any rock music fan knows. You simply curl your middle and ring fingers against your palm and hold them with your thumb while extending your index and pinky fingers. Interestingly, this same hand position, known in yoga as *karana mudra*, is employed in Buddhism as a means of purification and to banish obstacles, stuck energy, and unwanted conditions. It seems to be a universal gesture. Try it! I'm willing to bet you'll feel its power.

To deflect negativity using the sign of the horns/karana mudra, you don't even need to know who or where it's coming from. Using one or both hands, you can simply imagine that your index and pinky fingers are directing any and all negative energy straight back to its source.

Cloak

As I mentioned, when I first moved to a big city from a small town, I felt uncomfortably open to the stares and opinions of every person I happened to pass on the street. But I was also confused by how many people *didn't* look at me or acknowledge me. Where I grew up, it was common courtesy to smile and say hello, and to expect some sort of response in return. In a small town, passing someone on the street is significant: not only is the person walking by someone you probably know (or at least recognize), but such meetings also happen infrequently enough that a greeting does seem in order.

While I initially assumed that city people usually don't greet or even acknowledge passersby because they are distant, jaded, and cold, I soon learned that it's actually because there are just too many people to connect with in an authentic way, and it's draining to try! So it just isn't advisable to be that open on a crowded city street. Are some city people distant, jaded, and cold? Sure! So are some small-town people. But the way people act on the street has less to do with character and more to do with necessity.

Eventually, I learned how to close my face like I was closing and locking a door. When I was passing a stranger—even a stranger trying to get me to join their cult or making a comment about my body—I was able to look at them (or look past them) with the same closed face.

It was an invisibility cloak of sorts: not a cloak that made my body invisible, but one that made my soul invisible. That way, even my body didn't feel vulnerable to their stares, because, for all they knew, it was just *some* body, *any* body, not necessarily my body. But also, I felt literally safer because my closed face was broadcasting to the world something like, "You don't want to mess with me because you don't know who I am." I could have been a ninja for all they knew. And in many ways, I actually was practicing the ninja art of invisibility. People may have been seeing someone, but it wasn't *me*, as in my actual self.

But it wasn't just my face that served as an invisibility cloak; it was also my energy. Yes, there was a facial component to it, but it was also a whole body and aura sort of thing. Try it out. Look at yourself in the mirror in an open, welcoming, and possibly vulnerable way, and feel your body and energy field as

Basic Protection Techniques 53

open, too. Now relax your face into a poker face: shut it down. Feel the corresponding closure of your energy field around you.

Of course, I could remove the invisibility cloak if I chose. For example, if I ran into someone I knew or genuinely wanted to connect with someone, I could break into a smile and open up to them on an energetic level. Otherwise I could continue to wear the cloak for as long as needed.

If you are a born-and-bred city person, you probably learned to wear your "invisibility cloak" as a young child, through necessity or by watching your parents. So you may never have considered it to be a thing. It has always just been something you do. In this case, for our present purposes, it might be helpful to make it conscious. Notice when you're doing it, and feel the difference between when you have your cloak on and when you have it off. And the next time you visit a small town, if it feels safe to do so, try letting your guard down and see what happens.

But you certainly don't need to be in a city to wear your invisibility cloak! You can don it anytime you feel exposed or drained because you feel overly seen.

Concealing yourself by controlling your facial expression and energy field is one example of cloaking. You can also cloak your energy field and emotional openness by wearing silk over your heart, solar plexus, and sacral chakras. So basically this means wearing silk over your chest and belly. This is especially helpful for those of you who, like me, can get spooked or feel overwhelmed in crowds. (Are you noticing a theme? I'm sort of a hermit, aren't I?)

When you literally cloak your emotional centers with silk, you will feel less vulnerable and exposed, so you'll find you can move through a crowd without fear. If you prefer not to buy new silk for humane reasons, you might consider looking for a silk shirt or scarf at a thrift store. (You can cleanse its energy before wearing it by placing it outside in sunlight for a few minutes and then flipping it over and letting it bathe in sunlight for a few minutes more.)

When you're choosing an intention, it may be helpful to decide whether you'd prefer to radiate, shield, deflect, or cloak. Each method has its own benefits. While one intention might feel right to you in one situation, another might feel right in a different situation, or even in the same situation on a different day. Once you play around with each of these practices and get the hang of them, you'll intuitively know which one will best suit your needs on any given day.

And if you're still wondering just how to do this stuff, remember: intention is key! So is calling on divine support. And so is visualization. To put it all together: set your intention, call on divine help, and then feel/imagine/sense that you are putting the protection technique into practice. If it feels a little awkward at first, just keep showing up and doing your best. You'll get the hang of it in no time.

Chapter 5

Amulets

Once again, I'm starting a chapter with a definition: *an amulet is an object of protection.*

You may be wondering why I didn't get to the amulet section until chapter 5. After all, movies, books, and television shows sort of make it seem like protection magic is *all about the amulet…* so isn't it?

Nope! Honestly, protection magic is more about the stuff you already learned in chapters 1–4: your state of mind, your divine helpers, your intentions, and your visualizations. However, it is true that amulets can be employed to assist with all of the above. Certain objects—amulets—can serve as a reminder or focal point of your magic when you empower them with two things: divine energy and your clear intention.

Do you *need* an amulet in order to protect yourself magically? Most times the answer will be no. Sometimes, though, an amulet will be invaluable. (I'm thinking about a creepy interaction I once had during which I almost certainly would have felt extraordinarily uncomfortable if I had not had a clove of garlic tied into fabric and safety pinned to the inside of the center of my bra.)

There will probably be more times when you don't *need* an amulet but you still want one. Think of an amulet like a walking stick: You probably don't need one unless the terrain is steep and rough. But even if it isn't, you might want one anyway. It might make your journey a little easier and possibly more fun. At any rate, it won't hurt, so when in doubt, why not be prepared?

Amulets can be worn as jewelry, placed in a pocket, slipped into a drawstring bag and worn around your neck, or pinned to the inside of your clothing. You can even carry one in your hand, although that can often be inconvenient. The important thing is that you keep your amulet with you: on your person in some way, shape, or form.

Below, you'll find objects that are particularly suited to be used as amulets, along with descriptions of their magical properties and instructions for how to employ them.

How to Cleanse a Crystal

Before employing a crystal, you will want to clear its energy by cleansing it in one of the following ways:

- Place it on a clean white cloth, outdoors in sunlight, for 2–5 minutes.
- Place or hold it in a clean, moving body of water or under a running faucet for a minute or two (but don't do this with selenite, which will dissolve).
- Bathe it in smoke from a sage bundle, a palo santo stick, or a stick or cone of frankincense incense.

Additionally, if you're employing a crystal as a charm regularly, be sure to cleanse it using one of these methods at least once a week in order to keep its energy clear and strong.

How to Empower an Amulet with an Intention

To empower a crystal (or any amulet, actually) with your protective intention, hold it in your right hand. Close your eyes, take some deep breaths, and relax. When you feel calm and centered, call on the Divine in a way that feels powerful for you. Then feel your intention as if it has already manifested. For example, if your intention is to shield yourself from negativity, imagine you are cocooned in light, feeling happy, safe, joyful, and serene. Do your best to consciously amplify these positive feelings and invite them to swirl around your body, mind, and heart. Then imagine or sense all of these feelings as energy, and direct that energy into the crystal. Imagine the crystal (or other amulet) pulsating with the aliveness of your clear intention. You might like to finish with a spoken prayer or invocation, such as this:

> *Divine Spirit, thank you for empowering this crystal with bright, positive, shielding energy. While I wear (or carry) it, may I be safely cocooned in protective light. Thank you. And so it is.*

Minerals

Crystals and stones are popular in magic because each one possesses unique metaphysical properties that can assist with various intentions. To honor humans, ecosystems, and Mother Earth, it's important to find crystals that have been ethically sourced. You can inquire about sourcing methods at your local crystal shop or purchase ethically sourced crystals online at energymuse.com and thecrystallion.com.

The following minerals are helpful in protection magic.

Agate

You can find agates in many colors and varieties. All are protective. Agate helps ground you in the physical realm, so you feel safe in your body and aligned with the power of the earth. Of the four protective dynamics (radiate, shield, deflect, and cloak), agate is most helpful with shielding and radiating. Wearing or carrying it helps you broadcast strength and positivity, qualities that naturally support safety and strong personal boundaries. Choose agate if you want to feel solid, energized, and strong.

Aura Quartz

Aura quartz comes in a variety of colors and possesses many names: aqua aura, angel aura, tangerine aura, violet aura, and more. An aura quartz is a clear quartz crystal treated at a high temperature with a metal, such as platinum or gold, to create a shimmery, pearlescent appearance and often a vibrant, otherworldly hue. Because it does not appear in nature, not every magician loves aura quartz, but I do. In addition to being beautiful, it has a lot of power. For protection magic, aura quartz is extremely helpful with shielding: it can surround you in a high-frequency aura of joy. Aura quartz is an excellent mineral to carry or wear when you want to stay positive in a challenging environment, or when you want to stay in touch with your natural state of happiness and peace. All aura quartz varieties possess these properties, but if you're not sure which one to choose, go with whatever looks the most beautiful to you or otherwise calls to you the most.

Black Tourmaline

Black tourmaline is an essential protective stone to have on hand. It supports both shielding and cloaking intentions by absorbing and dissolving negative energy of all varieties. Simply holding a black tourmaline can disperse anxiety and neutralize frenetic energy. If feelings of vulnerability or restlessness keep you up at night, try holding or wearing a tourmaline while you sleep. Similarly, if you feel vulnerable or anxious during waking hours, tourmaline can seriously support you by keeping the effects of negative thoughts, feelings, intentions, and actions from entering your energy field and personal space.

Bloodstone

If you need to stand up for yourself or someone else in order to right a wrong or otherwise establish greater fairness, wearing or carrying bloodstone will help you wield power and influence in any situation by radiating confidence, enthusiasm, eloquence, and passion. With bloodstone, you will find yourself shining your light so brilliantly that it will be easy for you to get your way, provided your intentions are in alignment with the highest and truest good of everyone concerned.

Clear Quartz

Don't let the simplicity and abundance of clear quartz fool you: it's actually one of the most useful protective crystals out there. You can charge a clear quartz with any magical intention you choose, which means it can help with any protection dynamic.

In other words, it can help you radiate, shield, deflect, or cloak, or work with any combination of the four. Or, if your protective intentions might change at any point throughout the day (for example, if you want to deflect on your way to and from work, shield and radiate at work, and cloak during your lunch break), you can seamlessly empower it with various intentions as needed throughout the day. (Just be sure to cleanse it when you get home.)

Garnet

Perhaps more than any other crystal, garnet can help with cloaking. A stone with a strong, earthy, and passionate vibration, garnet can help us fortify our defenses so that we can move through the world with an outer protective boundary against drama, distraction, and discord, even as we stay inwardly connected to our emotions and empathy.

Hematite

A polished hematite is cool, smooth, and surprisingly heavy, with a reflective, almost mirror-like appearance. Simply holding a hematite grounds the body and centers the mind. In protection magic, it helps mitigate fear and assists with deflection. Wear a hematite pendant over your heart or hang a hematite on the outside of your front door to deflect ill will, envy, and negative energy of all varieties.

Howlite

If you've never held a howlite, you will marvel at how light and airy it feels. Howlite is an excellent ally for shielding: it can help you stay in a pure, clear, high-vibrating field of energy, to transmute negativity into blessings and to perceive the positivity or positive potential in any given situation.

Jasper

Iron-rich jasper veritably sings with comfort and joy. In addition to helping us stay grounded, energized, and confident, jasper is a master at deflection: wearing or carrying it (when it's charged with the intention to do so) can send all negativity straight back to its source. This makes jasper a helpful amulet to wear or carry when you know you must encounter a challenging person, group, or environment, such as a neighbor, office clique, or public event.

As a bonus, jasper is a master healer for the physical body. For this purpose, empower it with the intention to heal, then place it on, or wear it over, the area of your body that needs healing.

Lapis Lazuli

Bright blue lapis is a wonderful ally for your inner child and for children who feel vulnerable, anxious, or unsafe. It possesses a comforting, joyful frequency that restores playfulness, happiness, and inspiration. Lapis can help people of all ages to radiate positive energy and to have a positive energetic effect on their environment. Choose lapis when you want to replace feelings of fear, discord, or helplessness with creativity, harmony, and a sense of joyful possibility.

Pyrite

Pyrite is an anchoring, earthy stone that is an expert at both deflecting and cloaking. It also combats feelings of financial despair and lack by infusing you with a sense that your natural state is one of abundance, and it actually helps magnetize money. Work with pyrite when you feel exposed or unsupported in the physical world, and to protect and fortify your personal energy field.

Ruby

While ruby appears as a precious stone in fine jewelry, it is also available in polished form at a reasonable price in some rock shops and metaphysical supply stores. Ruby is a beautifully upbeat stone that bolsters the heart and infuses your entire being with happiness, optimism, and hope. It's an excellent amulet for radiating joy, even in the most challenging environments. Additionally, it swirls in qualities of love, creativity, abundance, and success.

Selenite

Selenite absorbs, neutralizes, and cleanses negative and frenetic energy, making it a useful ally to carry or wear. In wand form, you can wave it around your body for a vibrational detox and reset. It can help with cloaking by erasing anxiety, fear, and worry, thereby making it easier to dwell within an emotional and energetic invisibility cloak (as discussed in chapter 4). Cleanse selenite regularly, as it's highly absorbent. Just be sure not to use water, because it will dissolve! Instead, keep it on a sunny windowsill or bathe it in sage smoke often.

Smoky Quartz

If you're extra sensitive to the many mental and physical pollutants of the modern world—such as electromagnetic frequencies, sirens, and car exhaust, to name a few—smoky quartz can be a helpful protective amulet to work with. It works on the energetic level to mitigate the effects of these toxins, so you can feel clear, clean, energized, focused, and calm.

Sodalite

If your career is stressful, or if you are starting a new job and feel vulnerable or overwhelmed, sodalite can shield your energy by filling and surrounding you with a sense of confidence, capability, and strength. Sodalite can also help shield you from career drama related to competition and comparison, and it can help bolster your energy so you can radiate strength and confidence for job interviews and other important career-related moments.

Turquoise

A classic protective amulet of the Americas and the Middle East, turquoise helps shield, deflect, and cloak. It works on the spiritual level to keep negative energies and entities at bay, and on the emotional level to keep you grounded in and surrounded by feelings of safety, happiness, and joy. Turquoise works best when worn as jewelry, particularly over the heart, thymus, or throat.

Botanicals

In this section, you'll be learning about roots, fruits, woods, resins, blossoms, and leaves that possess protective properties. Botanicals can be used in protection magic as charms, incense, or essential oil. Below, you'll find instructions for employing a variety of plants in your protective magical work, along with the unique magical qualities of each plant and the specific parts or derivatives of the plant that are helpful.

While growing or responsibly wildcrafting your magical botanicals yourself yields the best results, this is not always possible or practical. If you purchase a dried botanical, you can empower it before use by placing the amount you plan to use in a bowl and holding it in bright sunlight for a minute or two.

No matter how you obtain your botanical, be sure to take a moment to send your intention into the herb (as described at the beginning of this chapter). Do the same with a stick or cone of incense before you light it. If you're using an essential oil, you can empower the entire bottle with your intention before use.

Angelica

As its name implies, angelica is aligned with angels and the angelic realm. Growing angelica in your yard helps create a protective aura around your home. You can add a tablespoon or so of dried angelica leaf to your bathwater to cleanse your aura, particularly if you feel like you've picked up any sort of vibration or energy that you'd like to release. Angelica root can be carried in a sachet as a powerful shielding and deflecting protective charm. Diffuse essential oil of angelica to create a harmonious atmosphere and to remove challenging or stuck energies or entities from a space.

Cedar

Tie nine cedar twigs together with hemp twine to create a charm of protection against curses, hexes, and baneful magic of all varieties. Safely burn it when you feel the threat has passed. Diffusing cedar essential oil or burning cedar incense creates a protective vibration in a space by aligning the area with divine energies and wisdom. Anoint protective charms with essential oil of cedar to activate, enhance, or refresh their power. You can also anoint the outside of your front door (and all doors that open to the outside) to protect your home from all dangers, visible and invisible.

Dragon's Blood

Dragon's blood resin, from the *Dracaena draco* tree, is highly protective and can be employed to keep all negativity at bay. Sprinkle a tiny bit of the powder under your doormat to ensure no person or spirit with ill will may enter. Burn dragon's blood incense around any interior or exterior space for protection, or burn it during any protection ritual for added power. Dragon's blood that has been expertly prepared as a perfume oil can be applied to the wrists for personal protection. To protect your home, you can apply dragon's blood oil to the outside of your front door. You can also use dragon's blood oil to anoint other protective amulets to keep their magic strong.

Elecampane

Use hemp twine to tie a little elecampane root into white cotton fabric, and carry the bundle or pin it to the inside of your clothes to protect yourself from challenging vibrations related to drama, gossip, jealousy, infighting, or office politics at work or in any group setting. You can also place a little of the root, along with sea salt, in a bowl or glass and place it in a room to absorb and mitigate such vibrations. Carrying a small bundle of elecampane root can help you to clearly detect dishonesty and attempts to manipulate, so it can be helpful with real estate dealings, car shopping, and any other situation involving transactions or negotiations.

Garlic

If I could use only one protective charm or ingredient for the rest of my life, it would be garlic. Garlic is like searing-white sunlight in botanical form. It has been said that garlic is not just aligned with Archangel Michael but is energetically synonymous with him. Garlic protects against negative energy of all varieties, including unhappy/unhelpful ghosts and spirits, energetic cords of attachment to other people or situations, people with negative intentions toward you, psychic vampires, narcissists, psychopaths, drama queens, and all forms of danger. I have employed a single garlic clove as a protection charm on numerous occasions, always with spectacular success. All you need to do is empower a clove and carry it, but (as I mentioned at the beginning of this chapter) I like to sew or tie one into a little cotton fabric and safety-pin it to the inside of the middle of my bra. To protect your home, you can cut a garlic clove in half and anoint the outside of your front door, as well as all doors and windows to the outside, with a little of its juice.

Lavender

Lavender is famous for being relaxing and sweet, so you may think it wouldn't put up much of a fight against negativity. Well, think again! The positivity that comes with the scent of fresh lavender, freshly dried lavender, or lavender essential oil is actually so potent that it's nearly impossible for negativity to share a space with it. Grow lavender outside your home, wear a scent made with lavender essential oil, or diffuse the essential oil in your space to disperse heavy, stuck, and challenging energy and to establish a formidable aura of positivity and joy. Lavender's effect is cumulative: it repeatedly fortifies your shield of good vibes, making it stronger and stronger over time.

Peach

I once received some homegrown peaches as a gift. After I ate one, I noticed that the pit was humming with positive energy. A little research led me to discover this passage in *Cunningham's Encyclopedia of Magical Herbs*: "Branches of the peach tree are used to drive off evil spirits in China, and also to root out illnesses. Children in China wear a peach pit suspended about the neck to keep demons away." To motivate unwanted ghosts to move along, try placing a peach pit in the center of each room and then opening all the windows and doors to the outside for a few minutes. (If you have animals who may get out, you can just open the windows.) You can also carry a peach pit for psychic and spiritual protection.

Pine

Burn pine incense or diffuse pine essential oil during protection spells or to establish high and pure vibrations within your space. Or place sprigs or boughs of pine around your home, on your altar, or on your front door for the same purpose.

Rose

Roses vibrate at the frequency of love and are therefore believed to have the highest vibration of any living thing. Fresh roses have an immediate and profound effect on the energy of a space, so it can be helpful to bring in a bouquet when an area feels dense, negative, stressful, chaotic, or unsafe. Fresh roses and angelic energy are in harmony with each other, so any spiritual work with angels can be strengthened and enhanced by the proximity of one or more fresh roses.

Rose Geranium

Rose geraniums and rose geranium essential oil are highly positive and immediately strengthening and balancing to the mind, body, and aura. Spending time with a rose geranium flower and inhaling the scent can fortify your energy field and help you radiate happiness and strength, as can diffusing or simply taking a whiff of the essential oil.

Rosemary

Malevolent magic and people with a hidden or unkind agenda will be dissuaded from entering your home if you hang a bundle of fresh rosemary on or above the outside of your front door. Add a sprig of fresh rosemary to your bathwater to cleanse your personal energy and fortify your aura. Diffusing essential oil of rosemary in your space can help strengthen your boundaries and energetic well-being.

Yarrow

Yarrow has a strong, bright, positive energy. Grow it around your home to create a protective shield, or tie dried yarrow into a muslin bag and hang it on or above your front door to keep negativity at bay.

Charms, Symbols, and Other Materials

The following charms, symbols, and materials can be employed as amulets. Once you've chosen what you'd like to use, hold it in bright sunlight for a minute or two to cleanse it. Then follow the instructions at the beginning of this chapter to empower it with an intention.

Bones, Antlers, and Teeth

Note: please do not kill an animal for its bones, antlers, or teeth, and please do not purchase these materials if they have been cruelly obtained—i.e., only purchase found or naturally shed materials. If you can find a tooth or a piece of antler or bone peacefully and without causing any harm, you can employ it as a protective charm with wonderful success.

A tooth from any animal has inherent protective properties. The same is true of antlers and bones (or pieces of antler or bone). Even a lost tooth from a child or kitten can be used as a protection charm, provided you empower it for that purpose.

Circle

As we've seen in previous chapters, your aura (or energy field) is a sphere, and encircling yourself with positive energy is a primary protective technique. That's why a circle is a fundamentally protective symbol. Wear or carry a circle charm as a reminder and enforcer of your divine protection and positive personal boundaries.

Divine Images

Images of gods, goddesses, saints, and angels—especially if you are drawn to them or they are sacred to you—can serve as potent protective amulets. Or, if you'd like to employ a divinity for a specific protective purpose, there are many who specialize. For example, if you're Catholic (or even if you aren't), Saint Christopher protects travelers, Saint Francis protects animals, and Saint Dymphna protects survivors of abuse and anyone facing mental health challenges. If you can find a small statue, image, or charm depicting a divinity or deity you'd like to enlist, first empower it as described at the beginning of this chapter. Then hold the charm and call on the divinity for help regularly to keep its protective magic fresh.

Elhaz (Rune) ᛉ

Runes are letters of an ancient Norse alphabet that was used for both magical and communicative purposes. According to Vervain Helsdottir in chapter 7 of her book *Modern Runes*, "Protection is the common thread that runs through all the distinct meanings of Elhaz." Indeed, this simple, ancient letter, which is reminiscent of a sheltering tree, antlers, or a hand, depicts protection in plentiful ways. And upside down, Elhaz looks like roots, which can provide a symbolic reminder of the countless ancestors you can call on for protection.

Eye

Have you ever felt vulnerable because you imagined (or knew) that others were watching you—that they had their *eye* on you? As a protective charm, the eye reverses this dynamic by keeping an eye on everything around you, mitigating feelings of vulnerability while vigilantly looking out for your well-being. An eye amulet is also a classic deflector, as it sends negative thoughts, feelings, and intentions directed toward you straight back to their source.

Hamsa

A hamsa is a Middle Eastern symbol that always depicts a hand and often depicts an eye or other protective symbol in the palm of the hand. If you've ever held up your hand to clearly communicate "stop," "don't go any further," or even "talk to the hand," you understand the energetic dynamic of the hamsa. To deflect negativity away from yourself, you can wear a hamsa charm. To deflect negativity away from your home and family, you can hang one on or outside your front door.

Horseshoe

While a horseshoe is popularly recognized as a good luck charm, its history as a protection charm is perhaps slightly less known. Iron is said to repel ghosts, malicious fairies, and other unwanted spirits, and iron horseshoes are nailed above doors, with ends pointing up, as protective talismans for that purpose.

Mirror

In feng shui and other forms of magic, a mirror is a classic deflecting charm. A mirrored pendant can be worn to send negativity back to its source, and a mirror can be placed on a front door or elsewhere on the outside of your home for the same purpose. You can even use a small mirror or mirrored tile on the inside of your home, but with the reflective side against the wall, ceiling, or floor (depending on which direction your challenging neighbors are in relation to you). But this is not an amulet to employ just for the fun of it. I only recommend using a mirror as an amulet if you have a neighbor, coworker, or other person who is giving you trouble. Otherwise, a mirror could create an issue where there wasn't one before (by arousing suspicion or unnecessarily disrupting the status quo).

Pentagram

Horror movies do the pentagram an injustice, because it's actually a highly positive symbol that can be used as a powerful protection charm. Symbolic of the inherent harmony of nature and the unifying intelligence that animates and sustains nature, the pentagram emanates divine clarity, balance, health, and strength. However, due to its unfortunate associations, it can in certain instances cause more problems that it solves, specifically when it's visible to anyone who may be upset by it. This need not dissuade you from employing it, however. If need be, you can wear or carry a pentagram in such a way that no one will see it, for example, by slipping a pentagram charm into your pocket or wearing a pendant on a long chain hidden under your clothes. To employ a pentagram for protective purposes, choose or create a charm that is point-side up, as this is the configuration that symbolizes the harmonious and constructive power of nature.

Prayer Beads

Prayer beads are not exclusive to Catholics and yogis. No matter what form your spirituality may take, you can employ prayer beads for protective purposes. Still, if you're shopping for prayer beads, the Catholic and yogic varieties (rosaries and malas, respectively) are the easiest to find. But you can certainly make your own beads, or empower any beaded necklace with mantras or prayers. Of course, if you'd like to work with a Catholic saint or divinity, a rosary would be appropriate, and if you'd like to work with a yogic deity and/or a Sanskrit or Gurmukhi mantra, a mala would be a natural choice.

Here are some ways to transform a string of prayer beads into a highly protective amulet:

- **Pray the novena.** In chapter 1 of his book *The Miracle Club: How Thoughts Become Reality*, Mitch Horowitz (who, incidentally, does not seem to be Catholic) suggests petitioning for any given intention by using the Miraculous 54-Day Rosary Novena. "In short," he says, "it involves saying a traditional Rosary prayer in two cycles: first, in petition of your request for 27 days, and second, in thanksgiving for another 27 days, for a total of 54 days."

    If this practice calls to you, find instructions for praying the novena that appeal to you online or in a book, and obtain a rosary you love. (For example, there are rosaries and novena prayers that are specific to certain saints and divinities.) Then choose a specific prayer request related to protection. This whole process is something of a commitment, but it will leave you with an extremely protective rosary.

- **Chant with a mala.** Most malas include 108 prayer beads, and saying a mantra for each bead once daily for 30–90 days can empower your mala with highly positive energy. Choose a chant that is meaningful to you or is aligned with a divinity, deity, or quality of energy that you'd like to invoke for protective purposes. For example, in Kundalini yoga, which I practice, the following mantra is chanted to create a diamond-white shield of protection around the aura:

> *Aad Guray Namay.*
> *Jugad Guray Namay.*
> *Sat Guray Namay.*
> *Siree Guru Dev Ay Namay.*

According to Ana Brett and Ravi Singh, in chapter 20 of their book *The Kundalini Yoga Book: Life in the Vast Lane*, this translates to the following:

> *I bow to the Primal Wisdom.*
> *I bow to the Wisdom through the ages.*
> *I bow to the True Wisdom.*
> *I bow to the great Sublime Wisdom, which will always prevail.*

Even chanting the simple seed mantra *Om* for each bead will create a highly positive resonance, and *Om Shanti* will help you radiate harmony and peace. (You can find a wealth of additional mantras on YouTube and on various yoga websites. You can also choose or compose an affirmation as a mantra, such as "I am safe" or "Peace is within me and all around me.")

- **Empower a smaller strand of beads.** Even a short strand of beads, such as for a bracelet or key chain, can be empowered every day for a particular length of time (perhaps 7 days, 28 days, 40 days, or whatever feels right to you) to create layer upon layer of protective vibrations. You could use a mantra (as above) or a simple protective prayer for each bead, such as this one:

Archangel Michael, thank you for protecting me from all harm, visible and invisible, in all realms and in all directions of time.

- **Establish your own unique prayer bead practice.** Find or create a strand of beads that feels right to you for your protective purpose, then empower those beads in any way you like. Just remember to choose a clearly stated protective intention, then invoke the Divine and focus your mind on repeating a specific word, phrase, or prayer for each bead. Repeat this process daily for 7–90 days. You might like to start the process on a new moon and continue until the next full moon, or continue for one full moon cycle (i.e., until the next new moon).

Whatever beads and empowerment practice you choose, remember to wear or carry the beads if you want to use them as a protective charm. You could also empower a string of beads to protect your car and hang it from your rearview mirror, or you could empower a bracelet to protect your child and encourage them to wear it when they leave the house. You get the idea.

Congratulations! You've learned the fundamentals of protection magic. You can now begin putting it all together. You can protect yourself on an ongoing basis and in a general, holistic way using everything you've learned thus far. But if you want to supercharge your protection magic for a specific situation or circumstance, one of the spells or rituals in the next and final chapter will likely do the trick.

Chapter 6
Spells & Rituals

Up until now, you've been learning about the energetic dynamics of protection magic, as well as the proactive and preventive practices you can use to bolster your everyday energetic safety. In this chapter, you'll discover effective spells and rituals you can pull out of your back pocket whenever extra protection is needed.

While you may be tempted to skim through chapters 1–5 or just skip ahead to performing a spell or ritual in this chapter that seems to fit your present purposes, be aware that a solid understanding and regular practice of the basics (as described in earlier chapters) will make any spell or ritual you perform exponentially more successful.

That being said, if it's an emergency, by all means, start with one of these spells! But then be sure to go back, when you can, and read the preceding chapters and practice the recommendations they contain. (Also remember to protect yourself in commonsense ways in the physical world and to ask for help if you need it, e.g., by contacting the police, a therapist, or a hotline.)

When working a protection ritual or spell, please keep the following recommendations in mind. These are aimed at the beginner, but it never hurts to revisit the basics.

First of all, before you cast a protection spell, I highly suggest that you cast a circle. This way, you will be cocooned in a sphere of protection while you work. A magic circle also helps contain the energy of your spell, sort of like a cauldron contains a potion as it brews. Then, when you release the circle (at the end of the spell), you will release this magical energy out into the world. If you already have a way of casting a circle that you like, go ahead and stick with it. Otherwise, here's a basic and effective circle-casting method.

How to Cast a Circle

Find a quiet place to work your magic where you won't be disturbed. An open space on the floor or ground where you can stand with at least 2–3 feet around you in all directions is ideal. Use a compass to determine the cardinal directions of your space, if you don't already know them. (There's a compass on most smartphones.) Then, if you'd like, you can place a white candle in a holder or a small representation of each element in each of the four cardinal directions. If you choose the former option, be vigilant of fire safety. If you'd prefer to select representations of each of the four elements, here are some ideas for what you might choose for each direction:

- **East** is aligned with the air element. A representation of air could be a feather, a stick or cone of burning incense on a holder, a paper fan, or something else that reminds you of air.

- **South** is aligned with the fire element. Ideas for your fire element representation include a lit candle in a holder (again, consider safety), an essential oil burner, or something else that reminds you of fire.
- **West** is aligned with the water element. For water, you might choose a seashell, an ocean globe, a chalice or glass containing a little water, or something else that reminds you of water.
- **North** is aligned with the earth element. An earth item could be a stone, a crystal, a small houseplant, a round plate or dish depicting a pentacle, a dish or plate containing a little bit of salt or soil, or something else that reminds you of the earth element.

First, make sure everything you will need for your ritual or spell is within your designated magical space (i.e., where your circle will be once you cast it). Face east while standing up straight in a comfortable way, with your knees slightly bent so you feel grounded and buoyant. Close your eyes. Relax and center your mind. Take three deep breaths.

Connect with the element of air. To do this, you might imagine the feeling of the breeze on your skin and in your hair, the image of clouds moving through the sky, or the sound of wind in the trees. Say:

Element of air, I call on you.

Turn toward the south. Connect with the element of fire. For example, conjure up the scent, sound, and warmth of a campfire or imagine the blinding brightness of the sun. Say:

Element of fire, I call on you.

Turn toward the west. Connect with the element of water. You might bring to mind the sound and image of the ocean and imagine the feeling of it rushing around you as you stand in the waves. Or you could imagine you are gazing at or standing in a clear mountain stream. Say:

Element of water, I call on you.

Turn toward the north. Connect with the element of earth. Ways to do this might include conjuring up the scent of rich, damp soil after it rains or the cool, dark silence of a cave. Say:

Element of earth, I call on you.

Face east once again. Imagine yourself as light. Send a column or root of light from your feet deep into the center of the earth, which you can imagine as a golden ball of light, like a subterranean sun. Plug into that light and feel it moving up and entering your body and aura. Send a column or trunk of light from your head up out of the earth's atmosphere and into the center of the sun. Imagine the sun's light as the diamond-white light of infinity and the cosmos. Bring the light down into the crown of your head and sense it filling your aura.

Straighten your right arm and point at the floor in front of you with your index finger. Imagine a laser beam of light extending from your finger, and use this laser beam to draw a circle of light on the floor as you rotate your entire body in one full clockwise rotation, connecting each of the four cardinal points along the way. When you once again face east and complete the circle, stand in the center of the circle once more, feeling protected and safe. Say:

God/Goddess/All That Is (or whatever name for the Divine feels best to you at this moment), I call on you. Thank you for keeping me safe within this sphere of light and for empowering my magic with glorious success.

Now you're ready to perform your ritual or spell. You can sit down or remain standing, feeling safe within this protective sphere of light. If you need to place a small table or chair within the circle for the sake of comfort or convenience, that's fine. Just be sure to do this *before* you cast your circle so you don't have to leave the circle at any point.

When you're finished with your ritual or spell, it will be time to thank the elements and release the circle. Here's how to do that.

How to Release a Circle

When your spell or ritual is complete, face north. Bring the earth element fondly to mind. Say:

Earth, you were here, and I thank you.

Face west. Think of the water element. Say:

Water, you were here, and I thank you.

Face south. Align briefly with the element of fire. Say:

Fire, you were here, and I thank you.

Face east. Imagine the element of air. Say:

Air, you were here, and I thank you.

Connect with the earth beneath you and the sun above you. Say:

God/Goddess/All That Is (or whatever name for the Divine that you like), you were here, you blessed my magic and lent it strength, and I thank you. Thank you, thank you, thank you. Blessed be. And so it is.

Now I suggest that you throw your arms up into a *V* shape, as if you are throwing sparkling confetti at the sky. This will help you release the magic you've generated so it can go out into the world and do its thing. Then spin your entire body in one full counterclockwise rotation to further unwind the energy and set it free. Next, crouch down and place your palms flat on the floor or the earth. Set the intention to allow any excess energy you may be holding in your aura to naturally fall into the earth. Know that any energy you need will stay and any extra will go.

Finally, it's a good idea to consume at least a little food and drink to bring you back even more fully into your body and the physical world. Carbohydrates are the best for this, so maybe a cookie, a granola bar, or some toast. (If you're not that hungry, even just a cracker or some dried fruit would be fine.) Beer can also be good for this purpose, but obviously that's not always going to be an appropriate choice. Good alternatives to beer include kombucha, selzer, and sparkling juice (but even water will do).

Spells and Rituals to Protect Yourself

Here are some spells and rituals to protect yourself in various situations. If you don't find one that fits exactly with what you're looking for, identify the one that resonates with you the most for your purpose and then adapt it to suit your needs. You can do that by changing the wording, visualization, and/or intention until it clicks for you.

Spell to Protect Yourself from a Bully, Stalker, or Otherwise Threatening Person

I'm going to put a commonsense caveat here: if you're being harassed or threatened by someone, first make sure you're doing everything possible in the physical world to keep yourself safe. For example, when necessary and appropriate, change your locks, install a security system, block the person on your phone and social media, and/or contact the police.

Next, if you have anything this person has given you in your home, whether it's a note, a piece of furniture, or a bottle of perfume, get it out (unless it is evidence or may be evidence in a future court case, in which case place it in a box, tape it closed, and put it in your garage, your basement, or a far corner of your closet). The point is, as much as possible, energetically remove this person from your home, or at least separate yourself from them so there is little resonance for them to latch onto. The same goes for your digital world: your inbox, text history, voicemails, etc. (Evidence can be placed in a folder or on a thumb drive to separate it somewhat from the rest of your online communications.)

Then you're ready to perform this spell. It's best to do it on a Tuesday, Saturday, or Sunday when the moon is in a fire sign (Aries, Leo, or Sagittarius) and between second quarter and full, but if it's an emergency, just go ahead and do it anytime. (Information on lunar phases and signs can be readily found online or in a calendar or planner.)

Gather these items:

- 1 small glass bottle (Essential oil size is fine, as long as you can remove any dropper top while keeping the cap.)
- Sunflower oil (from the cooking aisle)
- 1–2 drops essential oil of frankincense

Summon the fiery presence of Archangel Michael by saying:

Archangel Michael, I call on you.

Pour the sunflower oil into the bottle until it's about ½ to ¾ full. Add the drops of frankincense essential oil. Close and shake gently to combine. Hold the bottle in both hands. Say:

Thank you for filling this oil with your fiery, protective light.

Envision the bottle filled and surrounded with Archangel Michael's blinding brightness. Lightly anoint your forehead, heart, and belly with the oil. (If you have sensitive skin and you're worried it might get irritated, you can just inhale the scent while imagining yourself enveloped in fiery light.) Say:

Thank you for surrounding me with a fiery wall of light and protecting me from all harm, physical, emotional, and spiritual.

Envision bright fire surrounding and protecting you. Say:

Archangel Michael, thank you.

After closing your circle, anoint the outside of your front door with a little of the oil, then do the same to each additional door or window that opens to the outside of your home. If you can move around your home in a circle from the outside, move clockwise. If you live in an apartment or duplex or this is otherwise impossible, it's fine if you need to reenter your home in order to reach the outside of all windows and doors. And if you have additional floors, feel free to enter your home to reach windows and doors on those floors.

You can also anoint your car, your desk at work, and anything else you'd like to protect. You may like to carry the oil with you when you leave the house so you can refresh the magic as needed. Remember to call on Archangel Michael each time.

Spell to Protect Yourself from Overbearing or Dysfunctional Relatives

Before you magically protect yourself from a relative (or relatives), ask yourself:

- Have I tried speaking my truth?
- Is there an uncomfortable conversation I need to initiate with someone in order to honor myself in this situation?
- Have I set boundaries that feel right to me?

With relatives, it can be easy to assume that we know what they will say if we speak up about what we need. For example, you may have read the above questions and thought to yourself,

"No, because if I do, they'll just say or do _____, and then I'll feel _____."

And you may be right! If you speak your truth, initiate an uncomfortable conversation, or set a healthy boundary, they may say or do exactly what you're expecting them to say or do. Still, honoring yourself usually requires you to do this anyway. And who knows—they might surprise you! At any rate, once you've responsibly handled the situation by speaking up, you can decide if you want to move forward with working magic to protect yourself energetically or if you want to actually set a boundary, for example, by telling them you're not going to visit anymore until you feel respected, listened to, or seen. (Or maybe you want to work magic *and* set a boundary.)

In some cases, you may need to have a conversation not with the challenging relative(s) but instead with a partner or loved one who seems to be pressuring you or expecting you to spend time with the relative. In all cases, listen deeply to the voice within you to determine what is true for you and how you can honor that truth. This is pretty much never fun, but it always results in you calling back your power, which feels great. So keep your eyes on the prize.

Now, after you've taken all of this into careful consideration, if you still feel the need to magically protect your energy from one or more overbearing or dysfunctional relatives, this spell is for you.

It's simple: call on the Divine or a divine helper in any way that feels right to you. Then empower a black tourmaline (or piece of black tourmaline jewelry) with the intention to absorb any challenging energy coming your way from the family member(s), including any thoughts or expectations you don't want to pick up on or internalize. Then carry or wear it as needed.

If you happen to have a family member who is not just challenging when you're near them but you suspect is also draining or infringing on your energy from afar, simply carry or wear the tourmaline whether you're near them or not. You can even sleep with it. In time, the dynamic will be healed and you will not need to do this anymore, especially if you have compassion for yourself, take care of yourself mentally and emotionally, and practice a clearing and shielding meditation daily (like the magical hygiene meditation in chapter 2).

Spell to Protect Yourself in a City or Crowd

If you, like me, tend to feel overwhelmed by populous areas and crowds, be sure to read the "Cloak" section in chapter 4. And if you'd feel more comfortable with an extra magical boost, go ahead and perform this spell.

This charm will help protect you energetically, spiritually, and physically when you're in a city or crowd, so you can feel holistically safe and sound. All you need is a hematite pendant that hangs over your heart center.

Before you begin, empower the hematite outdoors in full sunlight for a minute or two.

After casting your circle, call on the Divine in any way you like. Hold the pendant in your right hand and say:

I radiate confidence.
I am shielded in light.
I deflect all that is not love.
I am wrapped in a cloak of security.
With the infallible help of divine light, I am safe.

Wear the pendant as needed, under or over your clothes.

Spell to Protect Yourself While Traveling

If traveling seems to unsettle you because you feel spiritually or emotionally uncomfortable in airports or crowds, see the previous spell. Otherwise, this charm will protect you while you travel by promoting safety, comfort, and ease. You can also gift this charm to a loved one you'd like to protect.

All you need for this spell is a Saint Christopher medal.

According to Judika Illes in her book *Encyclopedia of Mystics, Saints & Sages*, legend has it that "any day that you gaze upon the image of Saint Christopher is a day that you won't die or, at least, not suddenly and unexpectedly."

After casting your circle, hold the medal in both hands in prayer pose, close to your heart. Call on Saint Christopher and ask him, from your heart, to watch over your travels and keep you safe. Or, if you are gifting this charm to a loved one, ask for safety on their behalf.

Wear the medal as needed, or instruct your loved one to wear it as needed.

Spell to Protect Your Emotions and Energy

This spell is perfect for empaths or anyone who feels overly open and sensitive. Even if you don't know exactly what you want or need protection from, this charm will help you stay safe from invisible and emotional threats to your well-being.

For this spell, you will need:

- A clove of garlic, empowered outdoors in sunlight for a minute or two

Optionally (see below), you will need:

- ¼ cup sea salt
- 1 cup Epsom salt
- A few drops of lavender essential oil (or rose water in a mister)

If you already feel drained or your energy feels compromised, or you just want to recharge your batteries and strengthen your aura, begin by taking a warm bath into which you've dissolved the sea salt and Epsom salt. If you'd like, you can also add a few drops of lavender essential oil. If you don't have access to a bathtub, take a shower and mist yourself with rose water. (Or just skip ahead to the next paragraph and start with casting your circle.)

Cast your circle. Hold the garlic clove in your right hand. Call on Archangel Michael and ask him to protect your energy field and keep you safe from any and all invisible dangers, including challenging emotions, ill will, and anyone who may drain your energy. Feel, imagine, and sense Archangel Michael filling and empowering both you and the garlic with bright golden-white light in which only love remains and through which only love may enter.

Keep the garlic on your person (for example, in your pocket, around your neck in a cloth pouch, or tied in fabric and pinned to the inside of your clothes) whenever you need extra energetic or emotional protection.

Spell to Protect Yourself from a Gaslighter

The classic 1944 film *Gaslight* popularized the verb *gaslighting*, which means misleading someone by invalidating their feelings and/or attempting to convince them that they are crazy or wrong.

There are so many ways we can be gaslit by the people around us. Even the simple question "Why are you so angry?" can be loaded with disrespectful subtext, such as "What's wrong with you?" and "A normal person would not be angered by this."

Of course, it doesn't hurt to examine yourself. For example, staying with the above example, if you were to silently ask yourself, "Yeah, why am I so angry?" you may find that you have some very good reasons to be angry. Or when you examine the source of your anger, you may discover that it's related to something that happened in the past and not the present situation at all. Or the person asking you why you're angry might genuinely not know the answer and is asking in order to understand you better. My point is that not all uncomfortable exchanges mean you're being gaslit. But it can often be hard to tell, especially when the situation involves someone you spend a lot of time with or someone you esteem (or both).

If you're not sure if you're being gaslit, ask a friend or family member you trust to talk it out with you in person or on the phone. This can often bring a surprising amount of clarity. Then, if needed, perform this spell. It will help you recognize gaslighting and protect yourself from falling under its spell.

Here's what you need:

- A howlite (piece of jewelry or polished crystal), empowered outdoors in sunlight for 2–3 minutes

- An 8-ounce mister of rose water (available online and at many health food stores)
- 3–4 drops essential oil of rose geranium

Do this spell on a Sunday when the moon is waxing (between new and full). After casting your circle, hold the howlite in your right hand. Say:

Archangel Raphael, bring me clarity.
Archangel Michael, bring me strength.

Wear the jewelry or slip the howlite in your pocket. Add the drops of rose geranium oil to the rose water. Close the mister and shake. Hold it in your left hand and say:

Archangel Raphael, fill me with clarity.
Archangel Michael, fill me with strength.

Gently mist your aura by spraying around yourself 2–3 times. (Always use your discretion with essential oils if you have sensitive skin. If you don't feel it's wise to take the risk, you can simply open the bottle and waft it under your nose for a similar effect.) Feel, imagine, and sense a bright, protective sphere of light around yourself.

On days when you know you will see or interact with the gaslighter (or suspected gaslighter), wear the howlite and mist yourself with (or inhale) the rose water potion. You can also visualize the sphere of light and repeat the angel invocations as desired (inwardly if needed).

Spell to Protect Yourself from a Critical Person

Is someone constantly criticizing you and it's bringing you down? First, ask yourself if you would like out of that relationship and if it's possible to end it. If the answer is yes to both, no need for a spell! Walk out the door and don't look back.

If the answer is no to either or both of these questions, ask yourself if you've spoken up about this. Have you asked the person to stop? Have you shared with them how it makes you feel? Have you talked through the situation with a friend or spoken with an authority figure (such as a teacher or boss) who may be able to help? Protection magic is not an alternative to being assertive. It shouldn't be a silent, passive-aggressive way of dealing with conflict. So as uncomfortable as it may be, a conversation may be in order. (If this feels absolutely impossible to you, it may be a deep-seated pattern that a therapist could help you out with. Frankly, I'd start there before attempting to magic your way out of the problem.)

If you have explored all of this and still feel you must spend time with a critical person and therefore need to protect yourself from them, go ahead and do this spell.

Here is all you need for this spell:

- An aura quartz (any color you feel drawn to)

Cast your circle. Hold your aura quartz in both hands. Call on the Divine in any way you like and speak words from your heart about the type of protection you'd like. How would you like to feel in this situation? In what ways would you like to be protected? Speak as if you are talking to someone who loves you very much and can help you in exactly the way you need, because you are doing exactly that.

Wear or carry the crystal for protection from this person as needed.

Spell to Protect Yourself at Work

This charm will protect you from negativity of all varieties at work. Do this spell on the day of the full moon (or one day before or after).

Gather these ingredients:

- A pendant with a charm depicting a hamsa, a mirrored tile, or an eye (You can choose a long chain for the pendant and wear it under your clothes if you don't want anyone to see it.)
- A white cloth (napkin size is fine) or a white candle (if there's no sunlight)

Before casting your circle, go outside and spread the white cloth in bright sunlight. Place the charm on top of the cloth and let it soak in the sun for a minute or two. (If there's no sun on the day of your spell, warm the charm for a minute or two in the light of a white candle instead.)

Now cast your circle. Hold the pendant in both hands. Call on the Divine in a way that feels powerful for you and say:

Thank you for protecting me at work. Thank you for protecting my mind, body, spirit, and aura. Thank you for helping me to stay energized and positive, and thank you for deflecting any and all negativity straight back to its source. Thank you, thank you, thank you. Blessed be. And so it is.

Wear the charm at work.

Spells and Rituals to Protect Your Loved Ones

Every day, as part of my daily meditation, I ask the Divine to surround my loved ones with light and to protect them from all harm. I suggest that you do this too, particularly with children, partners, animal friends, and anyone else you'd like to protect. The following spells are for times when you feel you'd like an extra dose of protection. (If you are their caretaker, remember to take every possible and appropriate step to keep them safe in the physical world as well.)

Spell to Protect a Child

To protect a sensitive child and to prevent them from feeling worried, overwhelmed, or unsafe, try this spell.

Gather these items:

- A lapis lazuli (stone)
- A picture of the child you would like to protect
- A bit of hemp twine or white ribbon

Cleanse and empower the lapis lazuli stone outdoors in sunlight or by safely burning sage smoke around it. (Be sure to safely extinguish the sage if you use it.) Then cast your circle and begin.

Call on the Divine in a way that feels powerful for you. (Personally, for this one, I'd call on Mother Mary, but there may be another divinity, saint, angel, or name for the Divine that feels more resonant for you.)

While holding the stone in your left hand, speak words from your heart about how you'd like the Divine to help protect the child, such as:

Mother Mary (or Great Mother Goddess, etc.), please keep (name of child) safe from all harm, and help them to feel harmonious, protected, and secure. Help them to feel free to be playful and childlike, and not to absorb negative energy or worry from their environment. Help them to sleep soundly and to know that all is well. Watch over them always. Thank you.

In your mind's eye, see the child smiling and laughing throughout the day. See them radiating positivity because they feel so joyful and safe. Sense and know that they are safe and sound. Feel this reality and feel gratitude for it, as if it's already completely present and true.

Place the lapis on the child's photo and roll it up into a small scroll. Tie it with the ribbon or twine and keep the charm somewhere safe. (For example, you might place it on your altar or in a jewelry box or dresser drawer.)

Spell to Protect an Animal Friend

To invoke extra protection for an animal friend, gather these items:

- A small image of Saint Francis of Assisi (such as a statue or tile)
- A brown votive candle and holder
- An image of your animal friend

Cast your circle. Light the candle and ask Saint Francis to watch over your animal friend. Speak honestly to this kind spiritual helper about precisely the kind of protection you'd like him to provide. Thank him heartily.

Open your circle, extinguish the candle, and move the candle, picture, and image to your altar or another flat surface in your home (such as a shelf, counter, or table).

You can light the candle and invoke Saint Francis to protect your animal friend once per day for as long as extra protection is desired. You might consider incorporating this into your daily meditation.

Spell to Protect an Adult Partner or Family Member

There is no need to cast a protective circle for this spell (unless you want to).

You will need:

- Dried yarrow, empowered outdoors in sunlight for a minute or two and then ground into powder with a mortar and pestle or coffee grinder (You can substitute garlic powder or powdered rosemary if your loved one is allergic to plants in the daisy family.)

Ask Archangel Michael to watch over your loved one, then sprinkle a tiny bit of the yarrow powder in their shoes. (Just the smallest possible amount will do.)

Spells and Rituals to Protect Your Stuff

Our stuff is often more than just stuff. A dwelling is shelter and belonging. A vehicle is transportation and independence. Money is a means of securing comfort and everyday necessities. These spells protect the things that help us thrive.

Ritual to Protect a Home

For this intention, perform the Basic Home Protection Ritual in chapter 2.

If you feel your home needs an extra dose of protection, you can do this ritual once per moon cycle (i.e., about once every 29 days).

Spells to Protect a Car

For something as important as car safety, which is literally a matter of life or death, daily protection is in order. That's why every day, as part of my morning meditation, I like to call on Archangel Michael and Archangel Raphael to clear my car of all negativity and to fill and surround it with golden-white light. Next, I ask Saint Christopher and the angelic realm to watch over it and keep everyone in and around it safe. Then I do the same for my partner's car.

If you want to take this a step further, I suggest holding a Saint Christopher medal in bright sunlight for a minute or two and then hanging it from your rearview mirror.

To protect the animals in your neighborhood from being hit by your car, you can empower a Saint Francis medal in bright light and hang it from your rearview mirror as well. You can then ask Saint Francis to watch over the animals in your area and keep them safely away from the road.

Finally—you know I've got to say it—be sure to drive safely!

Spell to Protect Your Identity

Identity protection is so essential for all of us these days! So naturally, before you do any energy work on the issue, if you haven't already done so, take steps to protect your credit in the physical world. Once you feel your identity is as secure as it can possibly be, if you'd like to protect your identity in the magical realm as well, go ahead and perform this following spell.

Gather these items:

- A small metal lockbox with a key
- Angelica root (enough to almost fill your lockbox)
- An expired photo ID or a copy of your photo ID trimmed to ID size

Cast your circle. Fill the small lockbox with angelica root, and immerse the ID or ID copy inside of it. Visualize the box filled with divine, protective light before closing and locking it with the key.

Say:

Divine Presence, God/Goddess/All That Is (or whatever name you prefer), thank you for protecting my identity, now and in all directions of time.

Feel safe, and feel gratitude for feeling safe. Thank the Divine one more time and open the circle.

Spell to Protect Your Wealth

Before doing this spell to protect your wealth, here are some quick feng shui tips to help you prevent your finances from leaking away from you.

- First, fix any leaks in your home. I am talking about literal plumbing problems. Water symbolizes wealth, and leaky faucets, showers, spigots, etc., indicate and perpetuate leaky finances.
- Second, keep your toilet lid closed when not in use. An open toilet is a downward pull of energy in your home, so it can create a drag on your finances.

Now, if you feel further guided to protect your savings, income, and other forms of financial wealth so that you can both retain and expand your prosperity, this spell is for you.

You will need:

- A silver dollar (washed, dried, and empowered outdoors in sunlight for 1–2 minutes on each side)
- Potting soil
- A terracotta pot and saucer
- A small citrine quartz (empowered outdoors in sunlight for 1–2 minutes)
- A jade plant (You can either purchase one from a nursery or use a cutting from an existing jade plant. If you use a cutting, you will need to propagate it first by placing its stem in water. In this case, wait until it grows plenty of roots before transferring it to a pot.)

Cast your circle. Face north. Hold the silver dollar between both hands in prayer pose at your heart. Say:

This coin holds the wealthy, abundant energy of the earth, crystallized into form.
It represents all my financial assets and physical resources.
Great Goddess Gaia, element of earth, I thank you for all that I have.
Protect my wealth, expand my wealth, bless my wealth.
May it abide, may it multiply, may it grow.

Now put a little soil in the bottom of the pot, and then the citrine and the coin. Pot the jade above the crystal and coin, using as much soil as necessary. Sense your money as energy, and feel that it is safe and blessed by the fertile, verdant energy of the earth.

Say:

Thank you, thank you, thank you. Blessed be. And so it is.

Open the circle. Care for the jade lovingly. It will grow and expand throughout your life, so be sure to repot it as necessary.

Conclusion

In addition to taking meticulous care of yourself on every level (physical, emotional, and spiritual), always remember:

You have friends in high places.

Protection is your birthright.

Divine helpers are with you always: they only await your call.

Whenever you ask for divine assistance, it shall be instantly granted.

You are a beloved child of the Divine.

And you are safe.

Bibliography

Brett, Ana, and Ravi Singh. *The Kundalini Yoga Book: Life in the Vast Lane.* San Diego, CA: Raviana Productions, 2018.

Calista. *The Female Archangels: Evolutionary Teachings to Heal and Empower Your Life.* London: That Guy's House, 2020.

Campbell, Joseph. *The Hero with a Thousand Faces.* New York: Pantheon Books, 1949.

Carroll, Cain, with Revital Carroll. *Mudras of Yoga: 72 Hand Gestures for Healing and Spiritual Growth.* London: Singing Dragon, 2014.

Chevallier, Andrew. *Encyclopedia of Herbal Medicine.* London: Dorling Kindersley, 1996.

Cunningham, Scott. *Cunningham's Encyclopedia of Magical Herbs.* St. Paul, MN: Llewellyn, 1985.

Helsdottir, Vervain. *Modern Runes: Discover the Magic of Casting and Divination for Everyday Life.* Emeryville, CA: Rockridge Press, 2020.

Horowitz, Mitch. *The Miracle Club: How Thoughts Become Reality.* Rochester, VT: Inner Traditions, 2018.

Illes, Judika. *The Element Encyclopedia of 5000 Spells.* London: Harper Element, 2004.

———. *Encyclopedia of Mystics, Saints & Sages.* New York: HarperOne, 2011.

Lembo, Margaret Ann. *The Essential Guide to Crystals, Minerals, and Stones.* Woodbury, MN: Llewellyn, 2013.

Nagoski, Emily, and Amelia Nagoski. *Burnout: The Secret to Unlocking the Stress Cycle.* New York: Random House, 2019.

Raven, Hazel. *The Angel Bible: The Definitive Guide to Angel Wisdom.* London: Sterling, 2006.

Schucman, Helen. *A Course in Miracles.* New York: Viking: The Foundation for Inner Peace, 1976.

Shinn, Florence Scovel. *The Wisdom of Florence Scovel Shinn.* New York: Fireside, 1989.

Whitehurst, Tess. *Holistic Energy Magic: Charms & Techniques for Creating a Magical Life.* Woodbury, MN: Llewellyn, 2015.

———. *Magic of Trees: A Guide to Their Sacred Wisdom and Metaphysical Properties.* Woodbury, MN: Llewellyn, 2017.

———. *Magical Housekeeping: Simple Charms and Practical Tips for Creating a Harmonious Home.* Woodbury, MN: Llewellyn, 2010.

Printed in Great Britain
by Amazon